Call Power

21 Days to Conquering Call Reluctance

Gary Hoy

ISBN 1-9294-9613-3

Published specifically for the Direct Selling Industry by
Dream House Publishing, P.O. Box 2650, Broken Arrow,
OK 74013

Printed in the United States of America
10 9 8 7 6 5 4 3 2

DEDICATION

In memory of my father Edward Hoy.
Who sacrificed so much for his family.
I miss you, Pop.

CONTENTS

# Foreword

Socrates wrote:
"Employ your time in improving yourself by
other peoples' writings, so you shall come easily
by what others have labored hard for."

I believe that one of the most costly things in our society is that of the unfinished book. To let this one gather dust would prove that all too well.

I am thrilled and honored to have the privilege of introducing to you a book that, if studied and applied with purpose and vision, can literally empower you and your organization beyond what you ever thought possible.

I have had the fortune of working closely with Gary Hoy for over a decade. I have witnessed first hand his years of trial, error, practice, failure, and eventually victory. The pages you are about to read are the results of those years of work, thousands of phone calls, countless hours of humble counsel and the eventual joy of observing his friends and colleagues rapidly learn skills that took him years to develop.

For most people, the only thing that stands between them and great success is the size of their dreams and the belief that they can attain those dreams. I have, over the last twelve years, witnessed thousands of hope-filled, excited entrepreneurs with childlike faith, be reduced in moments, to a mass of fear and self-doubt following a few unpleasant rejections. That once friendly device called the telephone, loved since teenage, becomes, in a matter of moments, a monster standing between them and unlimited financial success. No more!

Like a powerful lever, the information contained in the following pages can help you develop in a matter of 21 days, skills and confidence that may have otherwise taken years. Thousands have already been empowered by Gary Hoy's system; and so can you!

I have heard stated by some of the most successful entrepreneurs in the marketing industry that 85 percent of what creates wealth in business are the actions of setting up appointments and sharing opportunities with others. If a man or woman cannot readily overcome the common fears of contacting and inviting, they will, and do, fail miserably. But what happens when those fears are replaced with confidence and enthusiasm? Fasten your seatbelts; you are about to find out.

"Fear?" You will ask yourself, "What fear?"
Success and victory for you, is on it's way.
Read, apply, and prosper.

Thank you, Gary, for this powerful gift.

James Timothy Tasker

# Author's Note

There are actually two parts to this book. Part I lays out a program to overcome call reluctance. This program—with complete instruction, scripts, etc.— works! It is unique, yet extremely simple in content. It does not favor background, income level, education, or any other pre-determined circumstance. I will not confront you with scientific theories or formulas, just proven strategies that can help you move forward professionally.

Upon completion of Part I, you will be ready to get started with the *Check Mark Program*.

Part II of the book is comprised of 21 daily readings, which will act as a companion to Part I. Read one section each day for the 21 days of the actual program. One day's reading might deal with the emotions of going through the *Check Mark Program*. The next day may touch on the traffic jam you were in on your way home. The sections are not designed to be all-encompassing chapters, rather a thought provoking perspective, that in some way can improve your outlook on life.

It is my goal to be your companion for the next three weeks as you make your way through this life-changing program. Let the journey begin.

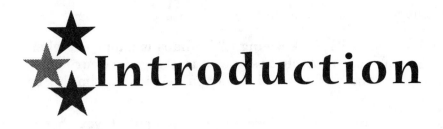

Introduction

Did you have a favorite neighborhood activity when you were growing up? Something the local kids gathered to play or participate in. In my neighborhood, it was street hockey. We would play every night during the week and twice on the weekends.

There was never a question of whether or not we would play, just how many kids would participate. I would like you to think of your favorite game or activity for just a moment. Recall what a fun part of your life it was growing up, as I would like to stir up a few memories in you to make a point.

I recall vividly going into the garage each night and grabbing my blue street hockey stick with the white plastic blade. I would then race off, meeting everyone in the street to play for what seemed like the entire evening. When we were done, I would put the stick in the exact same spot until the next day. Although I don't recall the specific games, I do remember how much I enjoyed playing.

As I look back now, however, I find it interesting that I cannot recall the last time I played. Usually when a part of your life changes, like graduation from high school or college, you remember the last day and even celebrate the occasion. It signifies a turning point in your life. Perhaps street hockey wasn't as big a deal as high school, but you would think there would be some recollection of the last time I did something which was a big part of my childhood. How about you? Can you remember the last time you and the neighborhood kids got together for your favorite childhood activity?

Years ago, I ran around the street with my blue hockey stick—for the last time. How strange I can't recall it. Someone scored the winning goal, the game ended and I put my stick in the garage—for the last time. Wouldn't it be interesting to see videotape of that moment? You bet, but you didn't tape it. You never thought it was going to be the last time. Life changed and your daily routine was soon mixed with other responsibilities.

Is it possible this similar type of moment happened with your dreams? When you were growing up weren't you filled with all types of ideas about a life filled with travel, good causes, big homes, and nice cars? This is not to say you haven't followed a successful path in your life, but did you come home one day and put your dreams away for the last time without knowing it? Perhaps it happened when you had your first child, took your first job, or signed a mortgage for your home? When these things happen, the world would have you believe it's time to be "realistic."

Of course, priorities change, but not to the degree you should put all your hopes and dreams away in a closet. I challenge you to think back on all the plans you had for your life and rekindle your desires to achieve them. It takes courage to do so, because it will make you uneasy about your present situation and how comfortable your life is today. That uneasy feeling, however, is the first and most important step to moving forward.

I begin the book this way in the hope that you will prime yourself to leave your comfort zone. It will take more than just the logic of the *Check Mark Program* to change your future. The first section of the book contains the actual program and the scripts to use in making your business contacts. So in effect, we are jumping right in to the guts of the book. Doing so can be risky if you're not focused on a dream or reason. The program you are about to get involved with can put a foundation under the plans you had when you were younger. My hope is you will not settle for what life gives you. Ask for more by getting your dreams and aspirations out of the closet! You'll rejuvenate those youthful emotions of awe and excitement for your adult life.

PART I

- ★ **The Check Mark System**
- ★ **The Scripts**
- ★ **Frequently Asked Questions**
- ★ **Personal Checklist**
- ★ **Script Companion**

Check Mark Program

To fully grasp the power of this program, you will need to flush all the preconceived notions of what you believe we are going to do. The ideas are a bit unconventional and may even go against some of the techniques you may have worked successfully in the past.

The focus of the program is to eliminate the fear of making a business contact by phone (sometimes referred to as "call reluctance"), which holds you back from exposing your business to others. The fear will disappear as a by-product of the success you have in attaining a "check mark" for 21 consecutive days. What you discover through completion of the program will astound you. There are components to this system that will be explained in the following sections. Do not take any of them lightly. Each has a specific intent in developing you into a contacting machine headed for an amazing lifestyle.

I am not implying you will have a full bank account in three weeks, only that you will begin to believe in greater possibilities. Activity, coupled with a belief in yourself will put you on course to change your financial future. There is a popular expression, "I'll believe it when I see it." Talk with any successful person, and they will tell you the opposite is true, "You will see it when you believe it."

The belief in your ability to create a successful business will be crystal clear after completing the program. Once the belief is there, it's only a matter of time before you see the results.

Where Does Call Reluctance Come From?

What was the event in grade school, high school, and college most feared by students? The test! Not because of the test itself, but because of the potential change in their life the results could produce. The actual test was only a piece of paper with some words on it. The ramifications of the test results created the anxiety. There are moments in our lives when we are met with anxious situations requiring performance. The exam came back with red marks on it highlighting what you did wrong. You were given a number explaining your result— 80 percent, 90 percent, etc. You did not get a number quantifying your effort, just your results.

Your performance, in effect, is depicted as either good or bad based on your results. This process is ingrained in us as we grow up, and follows us everywhere we go. You're in the top 5 percentile of your class. You came in second place in the spelling bee. You got a 92 on the big test.

I believe call reluctance is related to the desire for results. When we call a potential prospect on the phone (effort), we grade ourselves on whether or not we get an appointment (result). Unless we're a natural whiz on the phone, rejection is something we will face. The reluctance is developed through the mental picture of rejection. Without a successful experience, a positive mental picture is difficult to establish in your mind. The phone does not cause the fear—we talk on it every day. The potential negative result and perceived failure from the call, creates that uncomfortable feeling, which leads to avoidance. Notice in the figure on page five, all the available choices to avoid the phone, but where's the real problem? The roots!

There could be, and probably are, many more reasons for call reluctance. The one thing we know, however, is that fear exists when it comes to using the telephone. If you were to argue over the origin of the fear, that would be like having the flu and wondering if you got it from your brother or sister. Does it really matter? The point is you have it!

The Target: Fear of the Phone

A business that never gets exposure cannot possibly succeed, regardless of how good it is. The telephone is the best way to reach people, and it allows you to regulate your schedule at the same time. Proficient use of the phone, will allow you to book your calendar full of appointments without expending a large portion of your time.

The *initial* fear in talking to someone about an idea or business over the phone is what stands between you and consistent exposure. The fear is *temporary*—it does not have to last long. Get through the fear, and get on to the effort! When I mention effort, I do not intend to scare you away, just to prepare you for what's ahead. I doubt anyone reading this book is afraid of putting effort into a project, as most people are already working hard.

How many of you have put in 40 hours of work in a given week? Actually, most people work more than that. Moreover, if your spouse is also working, we're talking 80-100 hours a week per household. There's a big difference in working hard at a career, however, and dealing with emotional rejection. Let me share with you an example to clarify this point.

The emotional fear from a place of employment or business is usually in the first few weeks of work, and then, regardless of the time you put in, you are somewhat comfortable in your everyday routine. This is not to say things are always smooth, and you never deal with stress, but in general, you can go on autopilot.

After awhile, even contacting prospects by phone will become routine, although it can be nerve racking at first. The challenge is doing it consistently, allowing the repetition to eliminate the nerves. In order to eliminate the fear, we first have to acknowledge its presence. Most people find a reason to rationalize inactivity, when the real culprit is fear of rejection. The last thing someone will admit to themselves is picking up a little communication device scares them to death! It is time to recognize, and then conquer the biggest obstacle in your path to success—fear.

A great example of overcoming one's fear was depicted in a Disney movie a few years back called *The Mighty Ducks*. It was about a group of young kids who overcame insurmountable odds to win a hockey championship. The goalie, at one point, had a terrible fear of the puck, which was really hurting the team. The coach could have sat the goalie down and explained to him how effective his equipment would be in protecting him, but instead came up with a better method that involved actual experience.

He strapped the goalie's arms and legs to the goal posts, and let the team fire away. Helpless, the poor goalie was horrified. Shot after shot went slamming into his equipment, as he stood there motionless. There came a point when he suddenly realized through this *experience*, he had nothing to be afraid of because the puck didn't hurt. He was soon yelling at his teammates, challenging them to shoot the puck harder! Within a period of minutes, he was a new goalie.

When the straps came off and he was allowed to move, his teammates could no longer get a puck past him. He was full of confidence. Did he become a better goalie in a minute? The answer is yes, even though the talent was always there. The fear kept his abilities buried. *Once the fear was gone, his real talent came to the forefront.* The same holds true for you, except nobody is strapping you to the phone to face your fear. You must recognize, then face your fear until it subsides. Even though we can't strap you to the phone, I believe we can get similar results by completing the *Check Mark Program*.

If you are excited about your business, stop letting nervous tension camouflage this from a prospect on the other end of the phone. When fear is present, it is the first noticeable part of your conversation with a prospect. They sense it, and you feel it in your voice. When the fear is gone, the prospect will actually notice your enthusiasm, and you will become more effective on the phone.

The Process

Remove the perforated chart on page 47 of this book. I will walk you through the components of the program, then explain each in detail.

Notice the 21 boxes with stems coming out. This is where you will track the actual calls. The first row of boxes has five stems coming out of the top with little circles at the ends. The second row has five stems coming out the top, and two from the bottom. The third row has five coming out the top, and five coming out of the bottom. The little circles at the end of each stem are to be colored in for each call you make. If you are comfortable contacting people face to face, you can fill in a circle for that. However, make sure a majority of your contacts for this program are from phone calls.

The hexagon to the left with a "B" is filled in after reading 15 minutes in a *positive* book. The hexagon to the right with a "T" is filled in after you have listened to a positive tape at some point during the day.

After you have filled in all the circles surrounding a box, you've earned the right to place a check in the center. When you have a check mark in all 21 boxes, you have completed this life-changing program!

Why Does This Work?

The program works in a very simple way—by changing your focus. Notice there is no mention of setting up appointments, or selling products or services. Do not focus on results—concentrate on getting a check mark. Recall the example of the school exam. If all you had to do was show up and take the test (without having to score well), would you be as nervous? When the coach strapped the goalie to the goal posts, it was not to get measurable results. The goalie couldn't move, so how could he stop a puck? The purpose of strapping the goalie in was to face the fear long enough until the realization came there was nothing to be afraid of. I cannot overemphasize the importance of this. You are **not** attempting to meet tangible quotas; it's about filling your paper up with check marks, which means you are consistently facing your fear. The only requirement for you to pass the "test" is to receive a check mark each day (just show up!). Put all your energy into getting a check mark in that box! It will not be an easy process; in fact, it may be much harder than you think. It can, however, change your future.

Just as you invest in tuition for courses and seminars—you will be investing in your financial future by completing the program. You do not get tangible results from seminars and courses, rather information and experience to create results in the future. Treat this program the same way. The program's purpose is to face fear consistently until it subsides—not to bump your sales in three weeks.

You're not judged on the results since there is no measured performance other than a check mark. Each time you make a call you win! Eventually, regardless of how scared you were, the calls will be easier. The fear which once crippled you will subside. Enthusiasm and confidence will emanate from your voice. There is still work involved, however, the work will no longer involve an emotional punch.

Confidence is built on little victories, which is exactly what you will get every time you make a call. A completely new world will open up, as calling prospects will no longer be a big deal. The change will happen in your attitude, which eventually determines the success of your venture.

With each passing day, all the components of the program begin to shape you and your attitude. Pay close attention to every facet of the chart. Each one plays an integral role in creating momentum in your life.

Regardless of how excited you are about your concept, tension will show up when you're not comfortable with the phone. In essence, the phone fear not only keeps us rationalizing our inactivity, it limits the effectiveness of the calls we do make. By eliminating the nerves, enthusiasm is the first thing people will hear. When you communicate enthusiasm, people will follow. This will generate a momentum that will seem almost foreign to you. It is difficult to understand how easy it will be to pick up the phone upon completing the 21 days. Tension is replaced by excitement, and failure is replaced by triumph. Put a laser beam on that fear, and rid yourself of it for good! Only **you** can eliminate the fear through activity and repetition.

Can you see the difference in focus, compared to that of traditional goal setting? Simply get check marks in all 21 boxes. You will not recognize the way you feel and the power in your life, and neither will your friends and family. Gut it up and go for it!

The Dream Box (The Why)

The reasons you list in the Dream Box will be like gasoline in the fuel tank, because during the course of the 21 days, you may get side tracked, frustrated, or discouraged. In fact, it's likely you will experience a little of all of those emotions during the three weeks.

There is a tendency to get lost in the work and effort of any endeavor. The reasons you list in the box will help keep you focused. The following example may help explain the need for the dream box.

Picture a landmark in your mind, something like a sports stadium or museum that you have visited in another city (at least a few hundred miles away). If I were to make you an offer of 25 cents for each lap you ran around this landmark, would you do it? Keep in mind, you would have to travel out to the city and physically run around the landmark. Obviously, this would not be a good use of your time. If I upped the ante to $1 would you do it? How about $1.50 per lap? I doubt seriously that anyone would take me up on such an offer.

What if I were to change the reward to your yearly salary for each lap? In other words, you could earn thousands of dollars jogging around this particular landmark. Of course, people would jump at such an opportunity. The interesting part, however, is the work in any of the scenarios is identical. You would have to get directions, invest the time, physically get out of the car, and run. What changed in the last situation to make it so appealing? The reward!

Your reason needs to be the focus of the program, not the effort. Find things that move you emotionally, and list them in the box provided on the chart. A few examples might be: Spending Tuesday afternoon at the beach with the family, paying off your credit card bills and home mortgage, giving to your favorite charity, leaving your place of employment (provided it's a place you'd rather not be working), or attending your child's mid-afternoon play at school. Whatever you choose, make sure it moves you emotionally. The Dream Box will be different for everyone, but it's a necessary part of completing the program. We will talk more about the importance of a dream in the second part of the book.

Books and Tapes

The book and tape requirement will assure the flow of positive input into your daily routine. Too often people are stopped in their tracks by what seem to be insurmountable obstacles. Make sure this does not happen to you. Just like taking a bath, the influence of the books and tapes needs to be daily or it will wear off. This input will allow you to stay focused and positive during the ups and downs of the program. The books and tapes will guide you through the challenges, and pour gasoline on you when you're on fire! Unless you are different from everyone else on the planet, you will experience both.

As depicted on the opposite page, you can grow larger than your challenges by following a book and tape program.

There's an expression that says it all, "What's important is seldom urgent, and what's urgent is seldom important." Think of how many times you have talked on the phone for 10 or 15 minutes just because it rang. Books and tapes do not ring. Yet, they are filled with, as any successful person would tell you, important information. Fill in the "B" on your chart after reading for 15 minutes in a positive book, and the "T" when you have listened to a positive tape. There's a place for journals and business tapes; however, for three weeks, I would encourage you to utilize a book and tape program which focuses on personal development.

A note to those of you who highlight books, then simply review them on occasion. When you highlight a section in a book, you have obviously learned something. However, by the time you review that book again (and applied what you learned), you may grasp more of the book the second time because you have grown. If all you do is review the highlights, you may be leaving valuable lessons in the book. Every once in awhile it is a good idea to read a fresh copy of a book you review frequently.

Involvement in a book and tape program is of course optional. If you feel the need to pass on this part of the system, you will be doing yourself a great disservice.

A few words of caution—don't expect to like or agree with everything you read or hear on a tape. You don't like everything on a menu at a restaurant, do you? Especially in the beginning, treat the book and tape program the same way—look for something you like. Focus on what you can learn, not on that with which you disagree. As you begin to talk and work with people, you will have more experience with which to measure the information you're receiving from the books and tapes. Concepts and ideas you once thought ridiculous, suddenly make sense when applied to actual experience. Blending actual experience with the wisdom of successful people through books and tapes can turn you into a powerful force within the business world.

The Sacrifice

What you place in this section will vary from person to person. Some have plenty of time to complete the program, but might lack the funds needed to purchase the books and tapes. Others may have the money for books and tapes, but lack the time in their schedule to complete the phone calls. In both of these situations, you may need to sacrifice something in order to make room for the necessary resources.

If you are tight for time, analyze where it goes. How much television do you watch each week? Would 15 minutes of planning the night before help you find some extra time the following day? Does it really take you an hour to eat lunch? How important is that bowling or softball league? Somewhere in your week, you will be able to squeeze out the time to fill in your chart. However, it will not be without some type of sacrifice from your schedule. Successful people find the time to do what's important, even if it's inconvenient. The idea is not to *find* the time; you have to *make* the time.

If money is tight for the book and tape program, you'll also have to analyze where it goes. However, you can find the money, just as easily as you can find the time. Is your cable television bill making you any money? How much do you spend on junk food, soda, and eating fast food each week? Is there a chance you could live without season tickets? Could you give up golf for a little while? Many of these questions relate to situations that drain you of both money and time. The difficult part of finding the necessary resources is the manner in which you see your life. Certain things, such as television, have been eroding your time and money for years, but it seems to be a "necessary" part of your life, when, in fact, it isn't.

If you're feeling financial stress, you need to step back and realize where that stress is coming from—your finances! In order to improve your finances you will have to give something up. The equation usually works like this; if you want time with your family, you have to give up time with your family temporarily. If you want money, you'll have to invest money. Whatever it is you want, chances are very good you'll have to give it up for a little while.

Remember the sacrifice is not to deprive you of something you enjoy, but to allow you to fulfill the dreams you have placed in the *dream box*. The sacrifice section comes *after* you have written in your reasons. Before you decide to skip the program because you're not willing to sacrifice, ask yourself, "Is what's in the *dream box* more important than what I refuse to give up?" In other words, is softball or bowling more important than fulfilling your dream? These are tough questions, but ones you need to ask yourself because success will never be convenient. You will not have money fall in your lap by accident. There are no short cuts offered here. Your neighbors, friends and family might think you're foolish for sacrificing something, but they are not putting your kids through school, or paying your mortgage and credit card bills are they?

If you approach this program unwilling to give it the time and money it needs, the entire 21-days will be too inconvenient to finish. It will begin to tap your finances and time, and eventually your patience. Sit down and carefully analyze where your time and money are going. I believe you'll find what you need to get the program done.

Accountability and a Mentor

A key component to the 21-day program is the accountability created from the signatures at the bottom of your chart. Can you imagine what driving on the thruway would be like if we did not have traffic laws? Sometimes the law is not enough, and we need the police to keep us accountable. You will be aligning yourself with the laws of success when you undertake the steps in this book. However, you too, need a traffic cop-someone to help you stay in-line and focused on what you start. Allowing yourself to go "under the wing" of another person takes some humility, but another's perspective can be invaluable to moving ahead with your development.

Everyone needs a little nudge now and then, and by allowing someone to sign your chart, you are officially giving them permission to "push" when you need it. They will also be there to pat you on the back when things are going well.

If you are the type of person who doesn't need a nudge, check in anyway. It only takes one day to fall off the wagon. Perhaps that is the day having to answer to your mentor will keep you from skipping a day. I hope you'll take it on faith, that regardless of the type of person you are, having to check in will have a significant impact on completing the program.

Make sure you pick someone who has an interest in your success. They should have a background in the project you're involved in. The world is full of people offering free advice; make sure you get advice from someone who has what you are looking for in life, and a vested interest in your success. Do they have a life-style with a balance of time and money? If not, are they at least after the same things in life you are? There needs to be some common ground between you and the individual you choose.

Don't look for perfection, but try and have a general feel for their character and integrity. Trust your instincts and gut feelings, and you'll make the right decision. Remember, we are looking for someone who *willingly* wants to assist you, and is passionate about life and their profession.

Passionate people are often depicted as "fanatics." Do not be fooled by such a label. If you were going to have surgery, whom would you want operating? Some-one who is fanatical about the medical profession, or someone casually involved in medicine?

I hope that you have a few people who qualify to help you out. Pick one and get those signatures!

Upon receiving your check mark for the day, call your mentor and notify them. Voice mail, or email is fine for this notification. However, you should speak to each other at least twice a week. Be honest and up-front with your mentor, because they cannot help you if you do not fully inform them of what's happening. A fun part to checking in with your mentor might be a saying something like "Cha-ching!" in their voice mail. Using such an expression becomes a battle cry of sorts. We are working on a serious part of your life with this program, but you can have some fun with it too. As silly as that sounds, when you get your program up and cooking, the enthusiasm is contagious. Don't feel silly, share your excitement!

Some of the Benefits of the 21-Day Program

❖ You will learn from every call. Remember we are not going to put pressure on the results of the calls. However, even in the example with the goalie being strapped to the goal post, he stopped a few pucks even though he couldn't move. Similarly, some of your calls may produce results; consider this icing on the cake!

❖ You will have some real experience to run by your mentor. Someone else's knowledge is more valuable when compared with actual experience. Nobody can guide a parked car, not even your mentor.

❖ After receiving the check mark for the day, stop beating yourself up mentally for not doing more. You can enjoy the rest of your day knowing you have completed your task. The rest of your day will be guilt free. You cannot possibly understand this until you have gotten your first check mark. Being able to "turn the motor off" is a great load off your mind.

❖ When you get your check mark, you have a victory, regardless of any circumstance you face during the contacts. Even if everyone says "no," you still succeed. Remember the check mark is the focus, not the result.

❖ Should you start to develop new business from your contacts, do not stop contacting. If business shows up, great! You still need to press on and finish your program. This will prevent you from getting content with some results, and keep you moving. Creating too much business is better than creating just enough to keep you happy.

❖ When you do this program with other people, a synergy will be created which you cannot create by yourself. Do you think watching your home football team would be as exciting if you were the only one in the stands? Get together in a group and sign up to conquer the fear! I encourage you, whenever possible, to get 5-10 people started at the same time.

❖ When the fear of the contact has been eliminated, or at least tamed, you can now network more effectively. You will seek out referrals, because you will no longer be afraid to make the calls. Why would you ask for a referral, when the thought of calling on someone scares you? A name and number around you will be like a salmon in front of a grizzly!

❖ Getting the calls required for the day will challenge you. However, going through all the calls will certainly cause you to get your positive book and tape in for the day. That is a bit more mechanical, and something you may consider skipping. If you go through the discomfort of getting your calls in, I doubt you'll pass on the book and tape portion of the program which would prohibit you from your check mark.

❖ There may be a realization that you were not working as much as you thought. The activity of making the phone calls, and the potential results that may follow, will reveal much of the "work" you were doing before was mental, not physical.

❖ By overcoming a task that at one time scared you, your belief in yourself will grow tremendously. This will create a positive impact to everything you do.

What Happens After 21 Days?

First, realize the importance of momentum. If you have established a pattern of growth, do not stop the activities that created it. One of the biggest mistakes people make is sitting on past successes hoping to "hatch" new business. Especially when you have overcome a major obstacle (such as the fear of the phone), it is vital to stay in touch with the habits that helped you eliminate that obstacle. Embrace your newfound momentum, but do not lose sight of the way you created it.

Providing that you have not skipped any part of the program, when you're done with the three weeks, several concepts will become crystal clear. You will understand the power of a dream, the importance of sacrifice and commitment, the impact of books and tapes on your attitude, the power of setting and hitting a goal, along with the benefits of a mentor in your life.

Having experienced these factors for yourself, your ability to understand and subsequently teach them will be a priceless commodity. One of the best ways to learn is through teaching that which you have accomplished.

In addition, when a teacher begins to teach from actual experience, unlimited possibilities can develop through their mentorship.

We should be taught not to wait
for inspiration
to start a thing.
Action always
generates inspiration.
Inspiration seldom
generates action.

Frank Tibolt

The Scripts

There was a time when my hand shook and voice cracked when talking on the phone with a prospect. That experience was invaluable in coaching others to overcome the same fear. How could I understand fear in others if I never experienced it myself? Do not be discouraged if you have a hard time on the phone in the beginning, you'll get better. With enough practice, you'll become an expert. Weren't you nervous and somewhat unskilled the first time you drove a car?

A key point in developing a network of people is empathy for struggle. Look at the struggle as part of the process of becoming a great teacher.

Having what would be described as "the gift of gab" is fine, but it will not help you teach someone starting out on the phone for the first time. With the *Check Mark Program* and the scripts I share with you, *everyone* can become proficient at contacting regardless of their background.

The scripts are founded in simplicity. The simpler something is, the easier it will be for someone to begin and learn. The scripts will act as training wheels for a period of time, but eventually phone contacting will become natural. As effective as the words are in the dialogue, eventually you will put your own personality into the contact. The idea is to get everyone comfortable within his or her personality using the phone, not to create robots.

A word of caution, however—my words will work. I encourage you to use them. Since this program is grounded in simplicity, the *average* person can then duplicate them. Let me share with you an example of duplication. One of the most successful franchises ever developed is McDonalds. They have a system in place that has been duplicated worldwide, but the people who work at each restaurant have different personalities. They work within a proven success pattern that allows for differences in people. I would encourage you to approach the phone in the same manner, stay within the guidelines of the script, and understand your natural personality will become a part of your contact.

Before We Get Started

Before getting into the specifics of what to say, I'd like you to do me a favor. I have an idea that I'd like to get some input on. Turn the book upside down and to the best of your ability, read the next few sentences. As you're reading upside down, place one of your hands over one of your eyes. At this point, you should be reading the book upside down with one eye, while holding the book with one hand. Okay, now go back to reading the book the right way.

I have a question for you, was it easier reading the book upside down with one eye, or the more natural way? Your answer is not as important as the point I want to make from the exercise. People will do favors and give feedback! You could ask 50 to try this exercise, all 50 would do it—of course, some of you reading a book by yourself choose not to—but I hope you get the point. This is the foundation of the scripts you are about to learn—favor and feedback. The moment you ask someone to do you a favor, the "guard" goes down. Once that guard is down, the door is open for people to follow what you have to say.

Be aware the scripts will not put people in your business, or sell products. They will get you appointments with potential prospects. The fact that you're sitting in front of a prospect, however, does not guarantee business growth. You still need to be the catalyst that makes your business tick!

The following ideas are not *the* way to contact. They are *one* way to contact. The actual system you just finished learning about will help you overcome the fear of the phone with your dialogue as well (if you have one). What you are about to learn is the way I managed to set up appointments. I truly believe this method can work for you too.

Favor and Feedback

A request for help often brings out the best side of people. Chances are an individual would do everything they could to accommodate a request for a favor. Recall the last time someone stopped and asked you for directions. If you weren't able to help, you felt terrible, did you not? When you ask for a favor, you are appealing to the part inside all of us that wants to help someone in need. There are people to which this does not apply, but they are rare.

If the focus of your conversation is a favor, regardless of their ability to accommodate you, the response will be pleasant. This may go against your basic assertions of calling people, but for the goal of duplication, it is a much more effective way of getting started. It is especially helpful for those who have little or no experience in calling people on the phone. Someone with a strong personality can often set up appointments without asking for a favor, but can their personality be duplicated?

As was mentioned earlier, reluctance in making a call is often caused from a mental picture of being rejected. What is the mental picture of a person rejecting a request for a favor? An apology! Someone apologizing is a lot different than hearing someone get angry with you for calling. The less the phone calls "hurt," the easier it is to pick up the phone. That leads to more experience and eventually more results.

You will notice in the dialogues that follow, we ask for a favor (the word "favor" does not appear, but the tone of the dialogue implies it).

So, what is the favor we're asking? Fifteen minutes of their time to get an opinion (feedback). That is the goal of the phone call—face to face, for 15 minutes. If you attempt to impress them with information, they will invariably ask questions. When they ask questions, the focus turns to the business, and not the favor of 15 minutes in their schedule. As you will see in the scripts, just enough information is provided to get a person curious.

You will also notice there is a request for the prospect to give their opinion, or feedback, to an idea.

Why ask for someone's feedback about a business you know is solid? Regardless of how good you think the business is, whether they get involved or not will be determined by their opinion of it, not yours. Certainly, you can influence someone's opinion, but that's more likely to be accomplished in person rather than over the phone. Asking for feedback also tells the prospect you would respect what they think. For many, you will be the only person who asks for their thoughts the entire day! We're asking for a favor and an opinion; we are *not* providing information. Confused yet?

One mistake people make is passing on too much information on the initial call. The prospect thinks they need the information, just like a five year old thinks they can live on cookies! However, when you overload prospects with information, you provide them with material for questions. This in turn leads you to giving more information and the cycle never ends. A prospect cannot ask you a question about information that you have not given. Keep your focus on getting them to meet with you.

Information should be given face-to-face, and not through a question and answer session on the phone. Put yourself in their shoes. Which would you respect more, a business talked about over the phone, or one discussed in a person-to-person meeting? With practice, your ability to effectively set up appointments will be based on the atmosphere you create on the phone, not the information you provide.

As your poise and demeanor grow, you'll notice you have an ability to influence people naturally. It will have little to do with the words you use, and everything to do with the confidence you convey.

My little pooch, Silver, is an example of this principle. When he locks eyes with a deer, right away he wants to chase it. When he sees a cat, he is very cautious. Sure, he acts tough around the cat, but he is very hesitant to go after it right away. Logically you would think he would be more afraid of the animal that is ten times larger. However, a cat can radiate a confident "don't mess with me" attitude. Silver senses the fear in the deer right away, so he becomes aggressive and confrontational.

It may not make sense right now, but you will not have to answer many questions from prospects once you get some experience under your belt. What they need to know will come from the confidence they sense in your voice, not the "particulars" of the business model. Stay in control. Follow the scripts to the best of your ability until the words flow naturally. You will have to give them enough information to "wet their whistle," but anything beyond that is not necessary.

At the start, it will be my dialogue. However, within 3 weeks, it will be yours. As long as you are effective at setting up appointments, don't worry about the words. For example, Ty Cobb holds the record for the highest lifetime batting average in baseball history, and he gripped the bat differently than anyone else. There was a space between his two hands on the bat of about an inch and a half. Can you imagine someone going up to him and suggesting he change?

My voice shook noticeably for years as I pushed through the fear of the phone. As you overcome that fear, it's important to remember how you got there. When you become proficient at anything like setting up appointments by phone, others will ask, "What do you say?" Someone who repeats your words with nervous tension will not get the same results. They too will have to eliminate the nerves associated with picking up the phone, which can only be done through repetition and consistency. Make sure you include such information in any "how to" discussion with others.

The one sure thing is that the perfect script lies somewhere beyond the fear of the phone. Once past the fear, personality will take over and the appointments begin to roll! Even when you're nice and relaxed, always stay focused on covering what I refer to as the five flags. These flags do not necessarily apply to people you know (friends, family and acquaintances), rather referrals or "business" contacts. We will cover the dialogue for friends, family and acquaintances in the next section.

Five Flags

The "five flags" refer to the points you want to cover when you make a person-to-person phone call to a prospect. They are designed to set the prospect at ease and get an appointment. Each flag represents the sequential pattern of thoughts running through your *prospect's mind* the moment they pick up the phone. Too often people focus on information they want to convey, rather than paying attention to the prospects thought process. As you will see, when you've successfully handled all five, the prospect will usually utter the phrase "What is it?" or "Can you tell me more about it?" When you hear such a question, it tells you that the prospect is comfortable with the nature of the call, even though they don't know the specifics.

I will cover how we handle the "What is it?" question later. Let's first explain how we get to it. For the purpose of the following examples, I am going to call someone named John Smith from the XYZ Corporation. Remember, the flag represents what the prospect is thinking, not necessarily what they say. The phrase in the dialogue that covers the flag will be in *italics*.

Note: anywhere you see ***, represents a moment to pause. You don't want to sound like you're reading from a script, even if you are. The pause in the dialogue lets you create a conversational tone to the contact. Remember, we want to create a casual tone. The pause should be long enough for them to affirm what you are saying; something like "Okay" or "Alright" will usually come from the prospect. Here are the five flags:

- ❖ #1 Who is calling me?
- ❖ #2 Do I know you?
- ❖ #3 Where did you get my name?
- ❖ #4 Why are you calling me?
- ❖ #5 What are you selling?

Flag #1: Who is calling me?

John: "Hello"
My response: *"Hello, Mr. Smith, my name's Gary Hoy."*

Start with the prospect's last name. If you're calling a female and do not know if it's Miss or Mrs., use their first name only. We have an advantage when we call a male, because the "Mr." refers to all men. With women, you do not have such an advantage; therefore, use of the first name is going to be your safest bet, even if you lose the formal tone of the initial contact. For those who want to use the official term "Ms." feel free. If you look it up, that is a proper greeting, but you run the risk of someone being caught off guard because they may have never been referred to in this way.

Incorrect response: *"Hello, **John**, my name's Gary Hoy."*

Keep the greeting formal. Most people believe the use of a first name develops an air of friendliness, but again it is artificially created. This will always lead to suspicion. I am not suggesting John will say anything about this, but he will keep it in the back of his mind.

Incorrect response: *"Hello, Mr. Smith, my name's Gary Hoy, **how are you today**?"*

The bold section of this phrase is a common obstacle. What goes through your mind when a telemarketer asks "how are you today?" The first thought I have is "what are you selling?" Do not fill the conversation with artificial courtesy. John will spend the rest of the conversation waiting for the sales pitch, or what is commonly referred to as the "catch." In the beginning, we want to sound formal and respectful, not patronizing. The next flag handles their curiosity of where they know you.

Flag #2: Do I know you?

My response: *"Hello Mr. Smith, my name's Gary Hoy,* **you don't know me.***"****

This is the next question the prospect has, and until you answer it they will not hear another word you say. I have listened to many people on the phone give a beautiful explanation of what they're doing, only to hear the question at the end, "Where do I know you from?"

The flags must fall in order, each builds upon the prior one. Covering them out of order will not work; they need to fall 1-2-3-4-5. This will make more sense when you have finished reviewing all five. Flag #3 refers to the origin of the referral.

Flag #3: Where did you get my name?

My response: *"Hello Mr. Smith, my name's Gary Hoy, you don't know me.**** **I recently received your name and number on a referral**"

The purpose here is to let them know where you got their name. This is the next logical thought in their mind, and you need to answer it. If you have a strong referral, in other words, someone who the prospect knows very well and respects, use the person's name. It will lend credibility to your phone call. If you do not have a strong referral, just continue right past to the next flag without mentioning a name. By the time we knock out the next two flags, it will no longer matter who gave you their name.

Even if they know the person who referred them, do not stop. Keep going until you have knocked down all five flags. Talking about who referred you just throws you off and re-directs the focus of the call. Flag #4 gets to the purpose of the call.

Flag #4: Why are you calling me?

My response: *"Hello Mr. Smith, my name's Gary Hoy, you don't know me.*** I recently received your name and number on a referral,* **regarding some business projects I'm working on with some people out of the   (city/area)   and   (city/area) .**"****

The purpose of this statement is to gain some credibility with the prospect. There is security placed in their mind when you are not the only person involved, and you create a better image with some out of town connections.

You may be calling them from next door, but use some out of town credibility whenever possible. We are also introducing a business project in this section. The term "business project" is pretty generic and difficult to pinpoint, that helps us introduce a business concept without having to elaborate on it. The final flag lets the prospect know you're not selling anything.

Flag #5: What are you selling?

My response: *"Hello Mr. Smith, my name's Gary Hoy, you don't know me***. I recently received your name and number on a referral, in regards to some business projects I'm working on with some people out of _____ and _____ area***.* **I want to let you know right up front, John, I'm not a salesman or looking for an investor."*****

It is very important to mention you're not a salesman or looking for an investor, *before* you are asked. People are more likely to trust you if you give information without them having to ask for it. I personally do not consider myself a salesman, just someone looking for a business partner.

I think people need to qualify for your time. I look at a conversation over the phone as more of an interview. If someone responds in a positive manner, then I'll set up a meeting and educate them about my business model. I certainly will not sell them on the concept. My job is to share the opportunity. There is a time to sell products and services, but the initial call is not that time and not your goal.

If Mr. Smith asks the sales question first, regardless of how you view yourself or answer the questions, he will think you're selling something. You're better off covering this information before the prospect feels they must drag it out of you.

Notice I have used John's first name. Once you have begun speaking with a prospect, and established a respectful greeting, use their first name from that point on. A friendly environment is created when you remember, and use, someone's first name. To help you remember, simply write their first name in big letters on a piece of paper in front of you.

The complete dialogue looks like this:

"Hello Mr. Smith, my name's Gary Hoy, you don't know me***. I recently received your name and number on a referral, regarding some business projects I'm working on with some people out of the _____ and _____ area***. I want to let you know right up front John, I'm not a salesman or looking for an investor."***

Notice we have knocked down all five flags in a very polite and courteous manner. After the fifth flag, let the prospect say something. They will usually affirm what you have said with an "okay" or "yes," but make sure you allow them to say something since it breaks the one-sided nature of the conversation. The ground is now fertile for us to set up the appointment. The next phrase is where we ask for the appointment:

"I will be in the (prospect's town) *area next week* (or whenever you plan on being in their area) *and was hoping I could grab a cup of coffee with you and run some ideas by you regarding what we're planning on doing in the next 6-18 months***. I appreciate the fact that you're probably very busy, but if you could squeeze me in that would be great?"*** (Or, "I would really appreciate it?"***)*

At the end of the statement, we open the door for them to agree to meet. We are attempting to squeeze nothing more than a cup of coffee out of their schedule. You are finishing with appreciation, and a request for them to do you a favor. Notice how there is a question mark at the end of the statement. *If you do not pose your statement as a question, which can be generated by the tone of your voice, you will lose control of the discussion.* When you pose a question, they will give you an answer. If you offer only a simple statement, they will pose a question and create the direction of the conversation from that point on.

The ideal thought to create in a prospect is a combination of courtesy and a touch of opportunity. Many people are frustrated by what is commonly referred to as a "no-show." This occurs when a prospect does not show up at the scheduled time. Usually this occurs because there was too much emphasis on opportunity, and not enough on the courtesy. If the thought of the appointment is about an opportunity, they may decide they are not interested in helping you or anyone else make money. However, if the appointment was about doing you a favor, they will make more of an effort to get there. Through practice, you will eventually be able to decipher who will and won't show up. Then you'll have very few no-shows.

I once heard a successful businessman use a wonderful analogy about looking for potential business partners. He used a deck of cards, and explained how a phone call is like flipping a card from the deck. There are four aces in each deck of 52 cards. He compared the aces to the people you are looking for to build a business. When you use the above dialogue, if the person is an ace, they will meet with you based on the information you have supplied. The mistake people make is trying to turn everyone into an ace—you can't. The idea is to flip a lot of cards, because that will increase the chances of finding the right prospect. You control how many you flip, not what they are! The more you flip, the better the possibility you'll find an ace. The approach you are learning will ultimately reveal an ace.

Understand, nothing will work 100% of the time. Regardless of how terrific an opportunity you have, as you can see above, some people will not get it. Relax when this happens, because it's out of your control. Some people just don't get it!

At some point in your conversation, you will usually hear the prospect say, "What is it?" This question will come at the end of the five flags, or at the end of the phrase in which you go for the appointment. This should be music to your ears, as it tells you the five flags have been successfully covered. Especially if you are not working with a strong point of referral, the origin of where you received the name is no longer an issue. Your discussion will now go in the direction of the potential benefits of your business. Explain the benefits generically in order to get an appointment. The response to "what is it?" looks like this:

> *"Basically John, we're taking some of the technology available today and literally re-routing the way corporations are doing business in North America. All I want to do, however, is grab a cup of coffee and run the idea by you and get some feedback***. I appreciate that you're busy John, but if you could squeeze me in I would really appreciate it?"****

Always refer to what you have as an "idea." When you have an idea, it's yours. If you have a "business," the questions will come from the prospect to determine what type of business it is, as most can usually be categorized. The danger is the prospect drawing from a pre-conceived notion or earlier experience, and lumping you into what they believe to be a similar opportunity. If you talk about an idea, it is original to you and not comparable to other experiences the prospect may have had. Notice again, how we open up the door for the prospect to meet with us at the end.

Your answer to "What is it?" will generate one of three responses. First, you may get an appointment. Second, the prospect may not be interested. Third, you may create questions, as the prospects curiosity may have been peaked.

When the questions come, many make the common mistake of answering them. When you answer questions, the prospect follows it up with another one. Do not get drawn into a long discussion. The only question which needs an answer is the one you're asking the prospect; "Will you meet with me, and give me your opinion?' The more information you provide about your business, the further away you get from the purpose of the call; the appointment. So, if a prospect says, "Let's cut to the chase, what's this all about?" My response is consistent with the tone of my conversation since the beginning, *I was hoping you could grab a cup of coffee with me and take a look at an idea?"***

I have dropped enough information in the dialogue to let them know there's an opportunity sitting before them, but I have done it in a casual and friendly manner. At this point, if they are not willing to meet, I am probably not talking to an ace. The one additional line I use with people goes like this, *I don't want you to think I'm going to sell you encyclopedias or anything John, I was just hoping to get your feedback on an idea?"*** Usually the prospect will chuckle (no offense to the encyclopedia salespeople out there!) which can create a good environment for getting an appointment. That's all they'll get out of me. Notice, I go right back to the reason I called in the first place; favor and feedback.

As was discussed earlier, most people are friendly and willing to help. When you get better at using this dialogue, you will be able to separate the people who are worth putting in your schedule, and those who are not. I do not mention this to criticize those not looking to further their lifestyle in a business, just to make the time you spend away from your family and interests worthwhile.

The only interchangeable part of the script is who referred you. Everything else is systematically set up, and very duplicatable. Simply insert the name of the person referring you (if you have one), and continue.

Friends, Family and Acquaintances

Do not complicate what should be a simple process when you are using what is commonly referred to as a "warm list" (people you know). You can use the same basic ideas we just covered in asking them for a favor to give you some feedback. Something like this would work just fine:

"Hello John, it's Gary***. I'm kind of in a hurry, but I was hoping we could get together this week. I've got an idea I'd like to run by you, and would really appreciate your feedback on it?"***

The reason you do not cover the five flags is that the person knows you already. Going into great detail would actually be awkward, and cause more questions than anything else. Call to grab a cup of coffee, and don't complicate it! If the individual asks you some questions, cover them the same way we did earlier. Keep the five flags out of conversations with people you know.

Your perspective on calling people you know is very important. I often hear people tell me they feel as if they're taking advantage of their friends and family. Well, if that's how you feel, then you are! However, if you think for a moment of what building a network entails, your perspective should change. In network marketing models, your success is built by helping others succeed. Therefore, you're offering people your time and effort to help them make money! Do you think most people get that offer even once in their life? Unfortunately, sometimes people do not view network marketing that way. They are not stupid, but they are ignorant of the facts.

If a hundred people are wrong and one person is right, my question to you is "how many people are right?" Understand the value you are offering your friends and family, a chance to change their financial future.

The flip side to this is to let people say no. Pushing your business down their throat is not good for them or you. Have some faith in yourself and realize you don't need any one person, let them decide what's best for their family. Do not hesitate to call, however. You don't want them coming to you after you're successful and asking, "Why didn't you think enough of me to give me a call?"

The Electronic Ad Pack

Another form of contact is the electronic ad pack, or electronic advertising pack. This is a message left on someone's voice mail (or answering machine). *Not* an email. Sending email to people you don't know is useless, and in many cases, illegal.

The purpose is to leave a message that creates curiosity about what you're doing. Using the ad pack is like going fishing. The process of fishing starts by casting your line into the water with bait on it. You then sit back and wait until something bites the line. Once you feel the tug on the line, you begin to reel in your catch.

Leaving a message on someone's answering machine or voice mail is similar; cast your opportunity into the mailbox, and sit back and wait for them to bite! Do not go chasing this person if they do not call you back. That would be like an fisherman jumping into the water trying to put a fish on his line.

For this contact, having a voice mail system is important; otherwise get ready for your phone to ring off the hook! Here is a typical electronic ad pack.

> *"Hello Mr. Smith, my name's Gary Hoy, you don't know me***. I recently received your name and number on a referral from* (name of person who referred you) *regarding some business projects I'm working on with some people out of the _____ and _____ area***. I want you to know right up front, I am not a salesman or looking for an investor***. I'd like to get feedback from some people in the* (their city) *area regarding our plans the next 6-18 months***. I appreciate you're probably very busy, but I will be in* (their city) *area next week. If you could squeeze me in for a cup of coffee that would be great***. I apologize, but the best way to reach me is through my voice mail as I am in and out of the office all day* (Or, "traveling quite a bit"). *The number is area code (_ _ _-_ _ _-_ _ _ _)***. If you leave me a time and number to reach you at your convenience, I'll give you a call back and fill you in a little as to what we're doing***and hopefully we can grab a cup of coffee?*** Again, John, the number is* (area code and number). *Have a great day John, and I look forward to hearing from you."*

We have successfully covered the five flags. Notice the pauses are still in there, which may be even more important with the electronic ad pack. You want the prospect to hear a conversational message. That can be difficult when you are the only one talking.

Notice how I apologize for having to leave my voice mail. Nobody likes to talk to a machine, so I let the prospect know I understand this by being apologetic. They will understand if you tell them up-front. Oddly enough, most people would rather contact your voice mail, because they may be calling you at a time when a long phone conversation is not possible. This way they can leave you a better time for you to call and have a conversation. Also, leave your area code, even if it's the same as the prospect. This, similar to the out of town references, will give the business a bigger scope than just a local project.

Make sure you leave an appropriate greeting on your voice mail system[1]. I simply thank them for calling and ask that they leave a time I can get back to them in the next two business days. The greeting on your voice mail should be brief, and to the point. Do *not* get into specifics of the business you are developing. The greeting's purpose is to allow you and the prospect to connect on the phone, period.

---

[1] I recommend you have a voice mail system for the electronic ad pack. Otherwise, you will be disrupted during the day by return calls. I would also discourage the use of 1-800 numbers for callbacks. It associates you with infomercials and "no money down" business ventures.

I do not recommend using the electronic ad pack with friends and family. Leaving such a message would more likely create doubt rather than curiosity.

Advantages of the electronic ad pack are as follows:

❖ Voice mail and answering systems are accessible 24 hours a day. It will fit into your schedule, even if you can only call at 2am!

❖ The prospect will not be interrupted, and will get your "ad pack" at a point in the day they have set aside to check messages.

❖ You can usually re-record the message if you were not satisfied with it.

❖ If they call back, you know they are "qualified" for your business.

❖ You can usually get a good read on people from listening to the message they return to you, which helps in determining the caliber of prospect they are.

❖ You get an ideal time, number, and location to call them back. This is a huge advantage. They have picked the time rather than you interrupting them with a random call.

When someone responds to your electronic ad pack by leaving a message on your voice mail, the return call sounds like this:

"Thanks for calling me back so quickly, obviously there is only so much information you can leave on voice mail***. John, basically we're taking some of the technology available today and literally re-routing the way corporations are doing business in North America. All I want to do, however, is just grab a cup of coffee with you and run the idea by you***. I appreciate that you're probably pretty busy, but if you could squeeze me in that would be great?"*** (Or, "I would really appreciate it?"***)

It would be a good idea to use one phrase on your electronic ad pack, such as "I would really appreciate it," and then use the other expression on the call back, "if you could squeeze me in that would be great!" This way you do not repeat yourself.

I do not suggest using the electronic ad pack exclusively, because you need to speak with people to learn and grow into a successful businessperson.

Realize the telephone contact is a huge asset in building a big business. If you have an ability to contact people in person that will certainly help. However, since referrals will play a large part in your success, contacting a big list of people in person would be next to impossible, you would have to physically be around everyone on that list to contact them.

A final thought—don't get caught up in the mechanics of the contact. Persistence and repetition are vital components too. As you actively contact, your self-confidence will grow and so too will the number of appointments! Understand, nothing can replace the activity of making calls. When you *hear* something you forget it, when you *see* something you remember it, when you do something you *understand* it. All the material we just went over will never be understood until you get into action mode. Feel free to foul it up; I did for six years!

Handout Material

Many network-marketing companies use materials to share their business, such as videos, cassette tapes, CD-ROMs. One benefit to this is your ability to duplicate your business through consistent information, just as Ray Kroc did with his McDonald's restaurants. Of course, the key is you must be enthusiastic about the effectiveness of the material. If you're not, either change the material or don't bother using it. All good prospecting material has one thing in common; none of it has legs!

So let's discuss how to give your material the legs it needs to help your network grow. For the purpose of this section, I will explain the way I use a video (simply insert the handout information your organization uses when I refer to the video).

I do not recommend mentioning the video on the initial dialogue for the electronic ad pack. Keep everything the same when you leave the initial message. Sending a video to someone without talking to them first, reminds me of someone leaving a flyer on my car at the grocery store. Yes, it is simple, but also ineffective. *Therefore, the electronic ad pack script does not change, when using handout material, until the callback.*

The purpose of handing out the video is to share the concept with a "qualified" prospect. You may get excited about handing out a video the first few times, it's only natural. However, with experience, you will require the *prospect's excitement* before you part with any of your materials. If you hear any hesitation at all, it's time to move on. I would rather give one qualified person a video before randomly giving out ten. Remember the deck of cards and the four aces.

Electronic Ad Pack Call Back (Handout)

"Thanks for calling me back so quickly, obviously there is only so much information you can leave on a voice mail***. John, basically we're taking some of the technology available today and literally re-routing the way corporations are doing business in North America***.

> *Actually, we just put together a video that does a real good job of explaining what we're doing. Obviously, we're looking for a few people to work on this with us, but initially I was hoping you could just take a look at the video for me?"****

At this point you need to listen carefully to the answer. You have just lowered the bar for their participation, as they no longer have to schedule you for a meeting. If they don't jump on the offer of the video, that tells you a lot about their interest level. Remember, you're getting a check mark each day, so you'll have plenty of prospects to choose from. I mention that I'm looking for people to work with for a reason. It qualifies someone by letting them know there is work involved. In addition, it decreases the negative responses from people who watch the video and think I've misled them. When I mention I am looking for a few people to work with, that implies an invitation into the business, thereby eliminating any surprises when they watch the video.

If you get a positive response and they agree to watch the video, you're not done yet! This is what I say next:

> *"Terrific! Just so you know, however, I only have a few of the videos and several people who want to take a look at 'em, so I can only leave it with you for 24 hours. If you can't review it by then I'll have to get back to you later."* (An ace will not let you go!)

I use this dialogue in getting my video watched in 24 hours because it takes the pressure off the situation. You can certainly use other methods, but I find that people respect your need to get material back right away (*"I only have a few"*). There are other methods that require more assertiveness, but that takes many people time and experience to develop. As long as the point is made about a time limit, does it really matter how I made it? I have heard people say, "If you can't watch it tonight I'll have to assume you're not interested." That can make you appear "pushy" to a prospect. If they're home watching the video that night, as far as I'm concerned, the manner in which I get them there doesn't matter.

My final suggestion will be that they watch it with their spouse. The last thing you need is one spouse trying to explain the concept to the other one. If they watch it at the same time they will each get "pure" information. I accomplish this by referring to my need to get the video back right away, not by suggesting they aren't capable of making a decision on their own:

> *"It would probably be a good idea to watch it with your spouse in case they have any questions, because I do have to get it back right away."*

That may feel awkward at first, but you'll get the hang of it. As you're reading this, remember you're doing so without the experience. This will all make sense when you get into the arena!

Simply arrange to drop off the video and pick it up the next day. What happens next? When you pick up your video—*listen!* Then go from there.

Voice-to-Voice Contact with Handout Material

"Hello Mr. Smith, my name's Gary Hoy, you don't know me***. I recently received your name and number on a referral, in regards to some business projects I'm working on with some people out of _____ and _____***. I want to let you know right up front John, I'm not a salesman or looking for an investor.***

At this point you listen for their interest or curiosity. Cover the question "What is it?" the same way as we did in the earlier example, but change the last part:

"Basically John, we're taking some of the technology available today and literally re-routing the way corporations are doing business in North America***. *Actually, we just put together a video that does a real good job of explaining what we're doing. Obviously, we're looking for a few people to work on this with us, but initially I was hoping you could just take a look at the video for me?"****

The great thing about handout material is the speed with which pure information can spread through an organization. Think about it for a moment, if someone gets interested in your material, what do they say? Usually, "What do I do next?" How simple would it be to tell them to give the same material to the sharpest person they know? The simpler the process, the easier it is to duplicate. If you couple the *Check Mark Program* with proper handout material, the potential is there for an organizational explosion. If you have talents above and beyond the video process I just described, in other words you have great people skills and poise, can that talent be duplicated quickly? The key to fast growth is a system of duplication, not your talent.

For your friends, family and acquaintances the dialogue would look like this:

"Hello John, it's Gary***I only have a minute, but I was hoping you and Sue (Or, whatever their spouse's first name is) *could take a look at a video for me?*** It relates to a business project I'm looking at with some people out of _____ and _____. The video does a great job of explaining the project and I'd like to get your thoughts on it?"****

At this point, you will often get questions, which you can handle the same way we did earlier. Make sure you include the 24-hour time limit and the request for a couple to watch it together. Based on your relationship, whether it be a good friend or family member, the conversation is going to be different than with someone you don't know very well. Do your best to let the video or material provide the information, by avoiding long discussions.

People always ask me if it's easier with people you know or don't know. I think that all depends on the type of people you know. Bottom line, if the person you're talking to is looking for something, it's easier!

Finally, I can't overemphasize the importance of the 24-hour time limit. That is the most important aspect of using a video. Giving it to someone for only one day adds value to the material. The moment you give in to the "I'll need a week" response, you've assured your material a spot with the junk mail placed on the television.

Appointments versus Handout Material

If you're not sure which form of contacting works best for you—going for appointments or using handout material—counsel upline. You may find a combination of the two is a good idea. The knowledge and experience you gain from doing both, will help you guide others when you're teaching the process of contacting and inviting.

Eventually you will discover what works best for you. I have found it varies a great deal based on experience and circumstances (such as time, or distance from prospects). If your prospect is 300 miles away, qualifying them with some type of material might be a good idea before traveling all the way to see them.

The bottom line, however, is you and your upline should discuss your options.

You Need to Believe

If you follow all the above, yet lack belief in what you're saying, it will *not* work. There is no script available that will produce long-term results if you lack internal confidence. I'm not referring to confidence in your ability to set up appointments (that will come in time), I'm referring to the confidence in what you're saying. If you feel the words of the scripts are not accurate, adjust them to accommodate your concerns. If you have questions about your business model, get them answered.

There is no replacement for internal questions about the integrity of your "pitch."

The journey of ten thousand miles
begins with a single phone call.

Confucius Bell

Frequently Asked Questions

1. Your ideas and suggestions appear to conflict with information I am getting from my upline. Which advice should I follow?

    Make sure you follow the advice you receive from your upline. Although I am confident of the contents in this book, your upline is more familiar with your situation and business. I am not writing a book on the *only way*, rather a book on *one way* to succeed in a business of your own. Therefore, although I strongly recommend the ideas in this book, you should stay loyal to the people who have a vested interest in your success. If you find conflicting advice, check with, and follow your upline's counsel.

2. I am running out of people to contact, what can do I do about this?

    First, have the necessary list of names before you begin the program. This will eliminate scrambling for names (at least have the necessary five, seven or ten you will need for the next days check mark).

    There are several resources available to expand your list of contacts, such as high school and college yearbooks, wedding lists, and business publications. Using your local phone book can help as well. Browse the white pages by reading all the first names; this will jar your memory. Who do you know named Alex, Alison, Allen, etc.? You can also use the yellow pages, taking note of all the people you know in a particular profession. Who do you know that is an accountant, dentist, lawyer etc? Chances are you know more people than you think.

    If you cannot find the number or location of a particular person, type in "Yellow Pages" in the search engine of your computer. The Internet yellow pages will allow you to locate people via profession and zip code all over the country. If you're doing a meeting in another state, type in the zip code you're traveling to and a profession/occupation, and an entire list, with numbers and directions, will be generated on your screen.

    Other people are also a reservoir of potential contacts. As was discussed in the book, ask for referrals from people you meet with. If you're courteous and professional, even if a prospect is not interested, they may set you up with an entire list of referrals. Sometimes a "no" can lead you to hundreds of potential contacts.

3. I can't think of anything to put in my Dream Box?

    A point to consider is that dreams are often viewed as things we want. They can, however, be things we don't want as well. For example, if you're unhappy at work (and would like to quit your job), turn that into a positive force for replacing your income through a business of your own. Negative situations can be a great source of motivation.

    A simple way I get people pointed in the right direction is to list a few *obstacles* holding them back. These obstacles usually prevent the investment of resources into a business, which if successful, would create the financial freedom they desire. For example, time constraints (Church, coaching little league, softball etc.), or financial commitments (children's education, mortgage payments, credit card debt etc.).

    Chances are, what you look at as an obstacle, is the *reason* to move forward rather than hold back. Somewhere, rooted in your obstacles, is the motivation to get moving. Successful people often use what would be another's excuse, as their reason to succeed. For instance, desire for more family time can either be the reason you complete the *Check Mark Program*, or the reason you don't. The circumstance is not the key. The manner in which you view it is.

4. Do I have to check in every day with my upline?

    Yes. This is an important step of accountability. The need for it will be quite clear by the time you finish. You may need to be pushed by that accountability just one day, but it can make the difference in completing the program.

5. I am getting people interested with the electronic ad pack, and voice-to-voice contacts, but not setting up appointments—why is this?

    You are probably getting people interested with the "favor and feedback" foundation of the contact, but change the focus of the conversation when you attempt to set up the appointment. It's only natural to start feeding people with juicy information once you begin talking on the phone. However, it drifts from the premise of the phone call, the "favor and feedback" over a cup of coffee. Always remember why you are talking to people on the phone, to meet with them, not explain a business.

6. I have a quiet demeanor on the phone and sometimes feel intimidated when I talk with prospects. Is there anything I can do to improve my effectiveness?

    There will be moments when you feel intimidated by the tone and manner of the person you're talking to (even if you're a confident person). The line I suggest for this would be, *"This is something we're going to put together, we just don't know who we're going to work with yet."* This lets the prospect know you're serious about what you're doing and that it will happen with, or without, their participation. People often want what they can't have.

It also takes the focus off you as the leader of the project, because you use the word "we" twice. Of course, you can be the leader of a project, but we're concerning ourselves with what the prospect is thinking. If they think you're too quiet, or shy, to be a leader or businessperson, it's best to imply you're working with other people. Play the role of the "carrier" of the opportunity. The idea is to expose your idea through a meeting, not your leadership. You can establish that later.

You can portray a confident demeanor with words, attitude, or both. As you gain experience, you will learn the proper blend of what works best for you. Regardless of how intimidated, or soft-spoken you feel, you can be the one in control of the conversation with proper dialogue.

7. I am getting too many appointments (some that are not very good), is there anything I can do to alleviate this?

Yes. Within your script, add a few lines that "crack the door open" to what you're looking for. This allows you to either qualify, or disqualify the prospect before you schedule a meeting. A few examples of lines might be, *"Ultimately I'm looking to find a business partner, but initially all I was hoping to do was get your feedback."* This, at minimum, suggests you're looking for a business minded individual, without changing the purpose of the call.

Another line might be, *"We're looking for someone to help with the development of this project, but initially all I was hoping to do was get your feedback."*

If you're limited on time, in order to meet with real ambitious people, you may want to use this, *"I'm looking for someone who wants to make some money, would that be you?"*

You will get fewer appointments by adding qualifying lines, depending on how strongly you state them. However, the meetings you do generate can be potentially more productive. You can literally speak to people as if you are interviewing for a board of directors.

I do not offer many additional lines because you should not have to use many. Playing dialogue ping-pong with people, in my opinion does a disservice to your business opportunity. The last line I use is simply this, *"This is obviously not a good time for you, but thanks for your time."* The second a prospect hears this; they will know you're ending the conversation. An ambitious, or truly interested prospect, will not let you go without setting up a time to meet with you (or accept a video). Be willing to end the conversation and your prospect will reveal their interest level, if they have one.

I would also encourage you to avoid the, "I'll leave you my number if you change you mind" routine. When a prospect hears this, they're probably wondering if you have a napkin to wipe the drool coming out of your mouth! (Sorry for the bad visual). You are the one with the opportunity, do not degrade it by implying you'll jump as soon as they are ready (because 99.9 percent will never call you back). Perhaps the next time they are given an opportunity, they won't let it pass. You, however, need to move on to the next prospect.

Before jumping to the conclusion you should qualify everyone, don't forget all the potential positives that come from an actual meeting. You can always get referrals over a cup of coffee, or spark some interest with your enthusiastic presentation. The other benefit to a meeting is what you can learn about dealing with people. Ever time you have a meeting, you'll gain valuable experience in working with different types of people. This usually doesn't happen through a phone contact. You have to get a feel for your meetings and schedule to decide on what works best for you.

8.   People are not showing up for the appointments I make, or when they do, feel as though I've misled them. What should I do?

The answer is the same as in question number seven. Use some qualifying lines in your contact to sort out the more business minded and ambitious person. The exact same lines we discussed in question seven will work, although they are used for a different reason. By using the qualifying lines, your objectives will be more clearly stated which should prevent any concerns about misleading prospects.

Personal Checklist

Fill in the answer to the right of the question in the space provided.

Ability to set up appointments by phone? ____

1. Poor
2. Fair
3. Good
4. Excellent

Ability to set goals? ____

1. Poor
2. Fair
3. Good
4. Excellent

Ability to reach goals? ____

1. Poor
2. Fair
3. Good
4. Excellent

Attitude about my future financial situation? ____

1. Poor
2. Fair
3. Good
4. Excellent

My leisure time? ____

1. Do not enjoy it
2. It's okay
3. Very relaxing

This checklist is not to be shared with anyone— be honest with yourself

Contacting on the phone? ____

1. Scares me to death
2. Will not touch it
3. Bothers me, but I use it anyway
4. Doesn't bother me at all

I read positive books ____

1. Never
2. Seldom
3. Sometimes
4. Always

I listen to positive tapes ____

1. Never
2. Seldom
3. Sometimes
4. Always

I have a "spring" in my step at work? ____

1. Never
2. Seldom
3. Sometimes
4. Always

Teamwork is important? ____

1. Never
2. Seldom
3. Sometimes
4. Always

Counsel from others is important? ____

1. No
2. Sometimes
3. Yes

The phone is a "cashbox" for my future? ____

1. No
2. Yes

Totals score = _____ (numerical total of all 12 answers)
*Check the scale on the next page to interpret your score

SCALE

12 = Great potential

13-20 = Great potential

21- 30 = Great potential

31-44 = Great potential

Where you are has little to do with where you can go.

Script Companion

The Five Flags

- ❖ #1 Who is calling me?
- ❖ #2 Do I know you?
- ❖ #3 Where did you get my name?
- ❖ #4 Why are you calling me?
- ❖ #5 What are you selling?

The Dialogue

"Hello Mr. Smith, my name's Gary Hoy, you don't know me***. I recently received your name and number on a referral, regarding some business projects I'm working on with some people out of the _____ and _____ area***. I want to let you know right up front John, I'm not a salesman or looking for an investor."***

Ask for the Appointment

"I will be in the (prospect's town) *area next week* (or whenever you plan on being in their area) *and was hoping I could grab a cup of coffee with you and run some ideas by you regarding what we're planning on doing in the next 6-18 months***. I appreciate the fact that you're probably very busy, but if you could squeeze me in that would be great?"**** (Or, *"I would really appreciate it!"****)

The Response to "What Is It?"

"Basically John, we're taking some of the technology available today and literally re-routing the way corporations are doing business in North America. All I want to do, however, is grab a cup of coffee and run the idea by you and get some feedback***. I appreciate that you're busy John, but if you could squeeze me in I would really appreciate it?"***

"Let's Cut to the Chase, What's This All About?"

*"I was hoping you could grab a cup of coffee with me and take a look at an idea?"****

One Additional Line

*"I don't want you to think I'm going to sell you encyclopedias or anything John, I was just hoping to get your feedback on an idea?"****

Friends, Family and Acquaintances

*"Hello John, it's Gary***. I'm kind of in a hurry, but I was hoping we could get together this week. I've got an idea I'd like to run by you, and would really appreciate your feedback on it?"****

Electronic Ad Pack

*"Hello Mr. Smith, my name's Gary Hoy, you don't know me***. I recently received your name and number on a referral from* (name of person who referred you) *regarding some business projects I'm working on with some people out of the _____ and _____ area***. I want you to know right up front, I am not a salesman or looking for an investor***. I'd like to get feedback from some people in the* (their city) *area regarding our plans the next 6-18 months***. I appreciate you're probably very busy, but I will be in* (their city) *area next week. If you could squeeze me in for a cup of coffee that would be great***. I apologize, but the best way to reach me is through my voice mail as I am in and out of the office all day* (Or, "traveling quite a bit"). *The number is area code (_ _ _-_ _ _-_ _ _ _)***If you leave me a time and number to reach you at your convenience, I'll give you a call back and fill you in a little as to what we're doing***and hopefully we can grab a cup of coffee?*** Again, John, the number is* (area code and number). *Have a great day, John, and I look forward to hearing from you."*

Call Back

*"Thanks for calling me back so quickly, obviously there is only so much information you can leave on voice mail***. John, basically we're taking some of the technology available today and literally re-routing the way corporations are doing business in North America. All I want to do, however, is just grab a cup of coffee with you and run the idea by you***. I appreciate that you're probably pretty busy, but if you could squeeze me in that would be great?"*** (Or, "I would really appreciate it?")*

*Electronic Ad Pack—Call Back (Handout)

"Thanks for calling me back so quickly, obviously there is only so much information you can leave on a voice mail***. John, basically we're taking some of the technology available today and literally re-routing the way corporations are doing business in North America***. *Actually, we just put together a video that does a real good job of explaining what we're doing***. Obviously, we're looking for a few people to work on this with us, but initially I was hoping you could just take a look at the video for me?"****

*The initial message left for dropping off material in an electronic ad pack does not change.

Positive Response

"Terrific! Just so you know, however, I only have a few videos and several people who want to take a look at 'em, so I can only leave it with you for 24 hours. If you can't review it by then I'll have to get back to you later." (An ace will not let you go!).

Additional Suggestion

"It would probably be a good idea to watch it with your spouse in case they have any questions, because I do have to get it back right away."

Voice-to-Voice Contact with Handout

"Hello Mr. Smith, my name's Gary Hoy, you don't know me***. I recently received your name and number on a referral, in regards to some business projects I'm working on with some people out of Rochester and Syracuse***. I want to let you know right up front John, I'm not a salesman or looking for an investor***. *Actually, we just put together a video that does a real good job of explaining what we're doing. Obviously, we're looking for a few people to work on this with us, but initially I was hoping you could just take a look at the video for me?"****

**Voice-to-Voice Contact
for Friends, Family, or Acquaintances

"Hello John, it's Gary***I only have a minute, but I was hoping you and Sue (Or, whatever their spouse's first name is) could take a look at a video for me?*** It relates to a business project I'm looking at with some people out of _____ and _____. The video does a great job of explaining the project and I'd like to get your thoughts on it?"***

**Do not use electronic ad pack with friends, family, or acquaintances.

Qualifying Phrases

"Ultimately I'm looking to find a business partner, but initially all I was hoping to do was get your feedback?"***

"We're looking for someone to help with the development of this project, but initially all I was hoping to do was get your feedback?"***

"I'm looking for someone who wants to make some money, would that be you?"***

"This is something we're going to put together, we just don't know who we're going to work with yet."

21 Day Check Mark Program

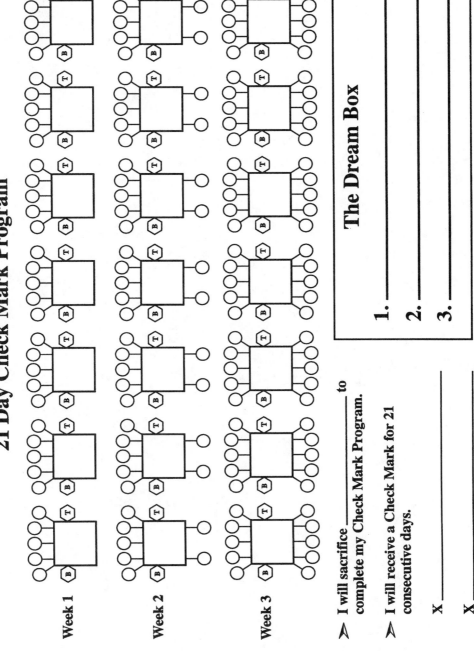

Week 1

Week 2

Week 3

The Dream Box

1. _____

2. _____

3. _____

≫ I will sacrifice _____ to complete my Check Mark Program.

≫ I will receive a Check Mark for 21 consecutive days.

X _____

X _____

Part II

Introduction

We all come from different backgrounds and in effect view life through our own personal microscope. Oddly enough, that does not separate us; it makes us similar to one another. Many times, I have come across situations where my convictions became stronger because someone challenged them. The ideas I touch on in the next 21 sections are all from my perspective, no matter how "correct" I believe them to be. If I can get you to begin thinking each day, regardless of whether or not you agree with my views, then I will consider this section successful.

Read one section each day for the 21 days of the program (this should supplement, not replace, the necessary reading to receive your check mark).

Make sure you limit the reading to one section per day. I love pickles and I love ice cream, but I don't eat them together! The daily readings will not necessarily connect with each other. Separate each section and chew on them one day at a time!

Dreams Make the World Go!

T he first dreamer that influenced me was the director of a school I worked at for nine years. We did not, and still do not, see eye to eye on much—but I have a great deal of respect for her. I figured she would be a typical boss, someone to tell me what to do. It wasn't long before I realized there was a special kind of drive in her.

She has a child with autism and wanted to build a school designed to meet the special needs of children like her son. At the time, the drive for "mainstreaming" was popular—an effort to consolidate all children under one roof. Therefore, her idea of a separate school was out of the question in the eyes of the state's education department. She had a vision, though, and began the fight. I do not know first hand the logistical struggle that took place. I only know she won. It took her many years, until the state granted her a license to open up a school. There was no stopping her, as she was fueled by a drive to help her son. She listened to "no" for years, but never accepted it. The picture of a school was etched in her mind's eye and she would not be denied.

The school opened with 15 students and a staff of 16. As the years passed, the student population grew to over 80 and the staff to over 100. I started my own company two years after I began working with the school. The concept of needing a dream to fight for in your life was becoming crystal clear to me, as working full-time and building a business at night took a great deal of energy.

My thoughts on this subject came up before a weekly Monday staff meeting at the school. There were about a dozen staff members in the room. I don't recall how the conversation started, but it was me against the rest of those in the room. I was taking the position that a dream was more important than having an education. Keep in mind this discussion was taking place in a school and the odds were not in my favor of swaying too many educators on this topic.

I was not criticizing education in any way, but I was trying to get everyone to understand the role a vision played in developing anything in your life. Finally, I stopped pushing my point on everyone and started to ask questions. I asked everyone to raise their hands if they had at least four years of college. As it turned out the average number of college years was about six.

Having laid the foundation for my point, I asked if anyone knew the one person at the school who lacked formal college training. Nobody was sure; they figured everyone had some level of schooling. I informed them there was, in fact, only one person (my boss) without college training. And she signed all the checks! That's right, the person who chased her dream of starting a school for her son provided the income for all the college educated staff. My intent is not to diminish education, but to help people understand the power a dream has in your life. Oftentimes, the higher up you go in a company, the less formal education you will find.

I recall a discussion I had with her one night about starting my own business. She simply said I could do anything I put my mind to, provided I had a reason to fight for it—the mechanics of what I was doing did not concern her. She knew with a dream anything could be accomplished. This is the type of advice you will get from successful people; they know it's possible because they are living proof.

Why versus How

Let's relate *How vs. Why* to something dear to your heart—the snooze button!

There are people who have no problem getting up in the morning (perhaps you should write a book for the rest of us?), and there are those who hit the snooze button four times! What happens when the alarm goes off? We instantly reach to shut it off by tapping the snooze button, and then roll back to our restful position. This is when the mind ping-pong begins. Lying there, your morning ritual unfolds in your mind. You run through a mental list of what you must accomplish before hitting the road to start your day. Most people will set the alarm 10 minutes before they have to get up-therefore the first tap of the button often times is a freebie. When the alarm sounds for the second time, it gets interesting.

We must begin to sacrifice morning activities if we are to get another ten minutes of rest. For everyone it will be different, but here are a few examples. As you lay there the first thing to go might be that second cup of coffee, or perhaps bacon and eggs becomes a bowl of cereal (didn't that article you read yesterday mention cutting back on cholesterol?). With this rationalization in place, we can safely hit the button again. In what seems like seconds, the alarm goes off once more and you reach over and tap the snooze. Hey, the weatherman said the roads would be fine this morning. The drive will be nice and smooth, so another ten minutes won't hurt—reach and tap! The next time we hear that annoying buzz we may decide to skip breakfast altogether, or decide the extra prep-time for that morning meeting is not so important. Of course there is always, "I got the kids up yesterday, it's your turn, dear."

Eventually this process leads to a point where no more minutes can be cut before it affects your day in an emotional way. Being late for things will inevitably affect your standing in the eyes of your co-workers or employees. That standing is vital to your financial future. The point is, the consequences of staying in bed begin to outweigh another extra 10 minutes of sleep—so you get up. Funny thing is, you knew how to get out of bed the entire time—just put your feet on the floor and stand! So knowing *how* meant very little, until the reason *why* became more important. As the consequences of starting your day late creep into your mind, the desire for 10 additional minutes of sleep no longer dominates your action. Did you ever wake up late and notice you dart out of bed? The emotional panic wipes out any tired feeling you would normally have.

This may appear to be a simplistic way of looking at motivation, but it points out a fundamental part of our being—we need reasons to motivate us into action. What separates the high achiever from the average achiever? The ability to develop a mental picture of something they want in their lives. That moves them to do what most people would consider "uncomfortable." The clarity with which this picture is seen creates an enthusiasm that is infectious and is reflected in their daily activities.

Many people will spend a good part of their lives hitting the snooze button, because they have already determined their future based on a company pension or retirement plan. Of course, there is nothing wrong with wanting to secure that, but I would challenge you to see more in your future.

Opportunity is everywhere and it comes in more attainable forms than winning the lottery. Think about the little line used to create a desire to purchase a lottery ticket: "All you need is a dollar and a *dream*."

When you have an internal reason to better your lifestyle, that reason will create the action. The action creates the results.

The difficult part is that all I did was explain the *logic* of having a dream or reason. Knowing it to be true and utilizing it's power are two different things. You may have to go search for a reason. Understanding the logic is a beginning, but I hope you will sit down and give some thought to what you're really after. When you figure out what it is that's driving you, write it down somewhere you can see it everyday (such as the *Check Mark Program* sheet). This will help provide the energy when you feel like hitting the snooze button!

If I had known my son
was going to be
president of Bolivia
I would have taught him
to read and write

Enrique Penaranda's mother

Day 2

Paul

Humility is a quality that will allow you to learn from many different people and situations in your life. I can think of no better way to describe this than to tell you about one of the students with autism I worked with as a teacher. His name was Paul. I was fortunate to be in a position to work with students in actual work settings within the community and Paul was one of my favorites.

One morning, Paul taught me the difference between experience and head knowledge. Paul is about as street smart as they come. When crossing a busy road, he would walk off the curb when the light turned green, knowing he had the right of way. If a driver did not understand that, they did when he placed his hands up in the air while in the middle of the street, as if he were Moses parting the Red sea, forcing the car to a complete stop. Then he would proceed at a leisurely pace to the other side. Very little doubt was in any motorist's mind as to who was in control.

Watching Paul clean at work was remarkable. The dirtier something was the more fun he had cleaning it. He's a confident and hard worker. His confidence would often get him in trouble, however, as Paul always thought he was doing things the right way (translation: Paul's way).

He had been taking care of his own transportation for many years by the time I had met him. He would either walk, or take the Metro bus everywhere he went. Independence was a big issue with Paul, although state guidelines are specific when it comes to what individuals with autism are allowed to do on their own while under our supervision. Therefore, Paul wanted to do things his way, the state wanted him to do things their way—and I got caught in the middle. Things were not exactly smooth at all times, but he had a lot of leeway with me, as I knew how street smart he was.

Paul was starting a new job that would require him to take the bus across town. There was nothing more exciting for him than a long Metro bus ride, followed by lots of dirty pots and pans! This trip was going to be a longer commute and required a different bus route from the one he had been taking. The state required constant supervision, counting on the "teacher" to be the one who would teach the "student" the ropes. I was the person assigned to complete the training, which was odd, considering I had taken the Metro bus only a few times. Therefore, it was time to get familiar with the schedule, rules, and regulations. I called the operator for schedule information and routes, so we could figure out which bus would get Paul to work on time.

After receiving all the appropriate information, Paul was convinced he had everything he needed. The standard answer from Paul came back, "I know," to every piece of information. He responded the same way to every statement regarding time, bus number, and transfer location. You have to understand Paul; you could tell him the price of tea in China went up $1.00 yesterday and he would say, "I know." Therefore, I was still a bit wary of his understanding of the bus route.

We were ready to go one overcast Monday morning, the teacher and student. The first bus was the same one he had always taken, so we hopped on that one about 8 am. That bus let us off about half way to our final destination, the school where Paul's new job was located.

We had a 15-minute wait for the next bus, which showed up right on time. When it stopped at the corner, rain now falling, we rushed from the cover of the terminal to board the bus. As the one who had plotted our course, I led the way. Curious thing was, Paul stopped just outside the steps and did not get on the bus. Having full knowledge of the schedule, I asked Paul to get on in a very firm voice—people were waiting in the rain behind him (rainy, gloomy Monday morning—the word "patience" was not applicable!).

Suddenly Paul started laughing and pointing in my direction, "Stupid teacher got on the wrong bus!" was the next thing I heard. As it turns out, the bus we needed to take was in fact across the street. The one I had boarded was headed the other way. The one with the *experience* was teaching the person with the *knowledge* the ropes. To fully understand any endeavor you get involved in, experience in the "ring" is key.

Paul taught a valuable lesson that day; knowledge will always come up short, when compared to experience. Certainly, a combination of both knowledge and experience is preferable. However, experience is, in fact the best teacher.

The greatest obstacle
to discovery is not ignorance—
it is the illusion of knowledge.

Daniel J. Boorstin

Day 3

Trust Your Stuff

I can recall pitching in, what I thought at the time, to be an important baseball game. Granted it was only at a local community league, but it was a moment that seemed so important at the time. I had been chosen to be a starting pitcher for the "big" game. The first batter I faced watched strike one, then proceeded to swing very late at the next pitch. I was brimming with confidence as I prepared to throw what I thought would be strike three. Unfortunately, pitch number three was deposited about 400 feet into a creek. I then proceeded to walk three of the next four batters, never getting out of the first inning. The following summer I took up a different sport.

Looking back, I know I did not stop pitching because I lost interest. What happened was my confidence vanished. I walked a few batters and had a very poor performance. Based on one pitch (and a ball that became very wet!) I decided, in my own mind, that I did not have the ability to throw a pitch in the strike zone that wouldn't get walloped somewhere.

Coaches in baseball often use an expression, "Trust your stuff" when young pitchers run into similar situations. It refers to the importance of having faith in your abilities. Pitching coaches will tell you their job is to develop the mental performance more than the physical.

It's only natural to draw back a bit from a setback or failure. Without the proper perspective, however, the setback can become permanent. Learn from it and move on. As I look back at my days as a pitcher, it seems so silly to have let one pitch change the direction of my interests. Granted it was only a baseball game, but do not lose sight of the lesson in the story. I never pitched again.

The same holds true for you when starting a business. You'll get knocked around. It has nothing to do with your ability, because it happens to everyone. Have faith in your business, but more importantly, have faith in yourself. Stay out there swinging! What you learn from your failures will develop the footing for your eventual success.

Where Does the Growth Come From?

One challenge in writing this book is sharing the empowering experience of successfully completing the *Check Mark Program*. Actually, there is no way I can get you to "feel" the results.

Let's say you had never actually seen the color red. I could describe it to you with all the words in the dictionary, and even take an entire week to do it. You may have an idea or two of what the color looks like, but it would really be a guess. It would be impossible for you to know, because you never "experienced" the color. However, if I flashed a red card for a split second, you would know. The actual viewing of the color would be done in a second, yet it would provide you with more understanding than a week of training could ever hope to.

When you blend your experience with the wisdom of others, you will grow. When you grow as a person, your business will grow, and not before. This is not a secret formula, but it is one many dismiss. I believe it is dismissed because personal growth is not measured in dollars and cents. It is not measured by what people say or by whom they know. In fact, it cannot be calculated by the naked eye. It can only be measured by the way one views themselves and their future.

The Same Holds True
for a Company You Create, or Work for

Technology is an ever-changing part of business. In fact, technology will often get credit for progress in corporate financial statements.

Ultimately there must be personal development (there's that theme again!) in the people running the company or business, to maintain any spike in revenue created by technology. Today, as much as ever, the ability to adjust to a constantly changing business environment is a vital part of progress. However, something that is new gets old, and if people do not grow personally with the "new and exciting"—stagnation may occur.

Companies are capitalizing on technology with websites and new promotional materials. This is a necessary investment to test the waters and keep pace with the rapidly changing world of commerce. You will often see an increase in enthusiasm, when enhancements are both announced and implemented, this prompts a very important question; is it the enhancement, or people's attitude about the enhancement that causes the growth in revenue. Could it be the bump in attitude creates the increase, more than the promotional enhancement physically improving the business?

If a company implements a new promotional tool or web site, their sales representatives begin to see an improved opportunity in their future and enthusiasm grows. It does not necessarily create an increase in activity, just an increase in the excitement of the existing activity. Too often, the expectation is that more results will come from the same effort. "I made twenty sales calls last month. This month's twenty should be even better because of the new web site!" The emphasis is on the new web site, not the improvement of the person (and their attitude) taking the new site to market. In the end, the new promotional tool becomes old. The initial enthusiasm runs out and stagnation creeps in.

Suddenly, everyone is looking around wondering why the web site didn't do what it was supposed to. Actually, the web site never did anything. It was growth in attitude, which created the flux in the first place.

We forfeit three-fourths
of ourselves to be
like other people.

Arthur Schopenhauer

Day 4

Finish What You Start

When you decide to undertake something like the *Check Mark Program,* stopping should not be an option. People often ask, "What happens if I miss a day?" The answer is simple, "You don't miss a day."

When you give yourself an alternative to your original commitment, you'll eventually take it. That alternative is usually dressed in a rationalization that avoids the discomfort and fear of finishing what you set out to do.

For many, setting the goal is not the difficulty; it's fighting through all the potential pitfalls to complete it, that's the problem.

There will inevitably be obstacles to any goal you set. How you look, and recognize that obstacle, is perhaps more important than the obstacle itself. In order to finish what you start, put obstacles on the table and figure a way around, or through them. Leaving yourself a back door can be dangerous to your financial health. Fighting through your challenges allows you the freedom to learn from your circumstances, rather than be controlled by them.

The goals you set should be tied to the *"why"* we discussed in Day #1. The goals are stepping-stones to attain that reason which drives you.

When you commit to finishing, you do it wrong until you get it right. The formula would look something like this:

Dream + Commitment + Struggle = Victory

We often wonder at the marvelous accomplishments of great athletes, business people, musicians, politicians, artists etc. If you examined their past routines, you would soon realize they followed the formula. You see the *victory,* but the rest of the components on the left side of the equation were present as well.

The wonderful thing about this formula is that it works for everyone! It's not a secret, but it takes courage to follow. When you hit a wall with the *Check Mark Program,* remember this formula. It will help guide you through the three weeks. Do not be surprised when you're sitting in front of the phone, wondering why you signed your name to a program which challenges you so much. The feelings you have are a sign that personal growth is just around the corner. Fight through your doubts and finish what you start!

Many of lifes' failures
are people who did not realize
how close they were to success
when they gave up.

Thomas Edison

Day 5

Sal

Is there such a thing as "constructive criticism?" I can give you my answer to that question by telling you about Sal.

He's a personable young man we worked with at our agency for about two years. He had a stuttering problem that would often affect his ability to communicate effectively. I have known him for about six years and he has always been involved in speech classes to help him with his stuttering.

Sal has been in several programs designed to eliminate his stuttering problem. They were all very reactive in nature, because they dealt with the external communication problem. In other words, the corrections were attempted after he spoke. Sal would struggle to say something without stuttering and then the speech teacher would try and *constructively* correct it. Sal, for several years, was dealing with a speech class each day that corrected his mistakes. Because the focus was always on the mistakes, failure was a constant companion every time he went to class.

Sal's confidence was very low, which actually caused him to stutter even more. It created a vicious cycle of activity. The more he stuttered, the more correction he received. With one exception, he stuttered around everyone I have ever seen him talk to, including myself. The only situation where he did not stutter was when he talked to his horse. The horse didn't correct him, or judge anything that came out of his mouth. Sal had plenty of confidence around animals because they gave him unconditional love, not correction.

I am not suggesting the people who worked with Sal didn't love him. I know all too well that they did. Unfortunately, they were not building his confidence, and as a result, reinforced the very thing they were trying to cure him of. His stuttering was caused by a lack of confidence in talking with people, not because he didn't know how to speak fluently, but because people always corrected him. He proved he could speak perfectly fine whenever he had a conversation with his horse, so ability was not the issue.

I think this situation is testimony to the damage criticism can do to people, even if it's described as constructive. Be an encourager, not a person who finds faults.

When you instill confidence in people, despite their errors and shortcomings, you will truly become a constructive force in their lives. Notice in the cartoon on the next page, that you could walk through the garden and attempt to fix every flower, or you could simply turn on the water and nourish them all.

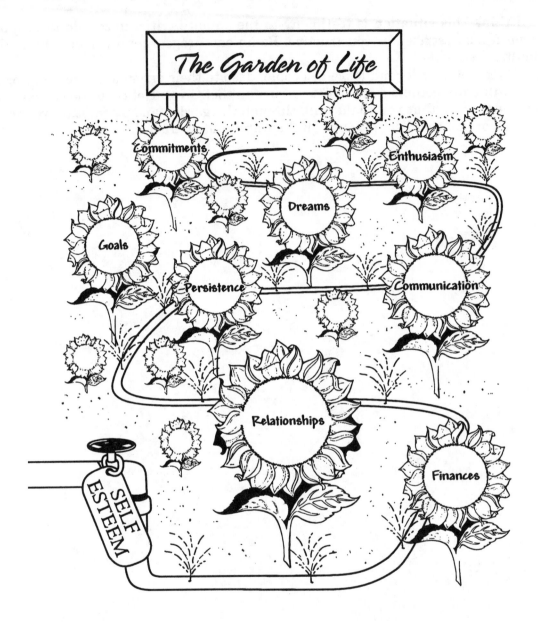

The Garden of Life

Day 6

Baby Steps Before Big Steps

I recall reading several chapters in a book about goal setting, which inspired me to write, what I thought were attainable financial objectives. Although I don't remember the exact figures, I recall thinking how nice it felt to write down some goals.

Unfortunately, I became discouraged less than a month into my plan. The problem wasn't lack of effort, because I worked hard, it was lack of results.

The goals I set were measured in dollars (income), not the amount of effort I put in. I did the work, but that didn't create the financial increase I planned for. Therefore I began wondering what good is it to set goals? I figured out one of the reasons people didn't set goals, it was frustrating!

The mistake I made was measuring just productivity, because I needed other people's help (through sales) to hit my goals. There are times when you can't control what other people do, but you can control what you do.

For example, suppose you set a goal to lose 25 lbs. in five months. This would require you to drop five pounds per month. What happens when you step on the scale after 30 days and you have not lost a pound? You might get discouraged, just as I did after the first month of my financial plan. However, if you put activity goals in as a foundation to the ultimate goal of losing the 25 lbs., your focus could remain even though your plan must be adjusted.

What you failed in was not dropping the weight, but in calculating the *activities* it would take to lose the weight. For instance, you could require yourself to exercise 25 minutes a day, rather than 15. Perhaps skipping dessert at dinnertime could be added to your plan.

This way you concentrate on the little steps *you control* in order to reach the ultimate goal (25 lbs. in five months). You haven't changed the objective of losing the weight, you have changed your mental focus and adjusted the activity to get there!

It works the same way in business. If you begin by setting goals which you control, such as number of phone calls or contacts each day, eventually you get a bearing on what it takes to reach productivity goals.

Performing the little steps everyday will boost belief. This relates directly to setting new goals. A snowball effect develops as your increased confidence factors into any new goals you might set in the future.

The *Check Mark Program* is an example of an activity goal. Only you determine if a check mark is received that day, nobody else needs to participate.

It is always wise to get some advice (like the person who signed your chart) before determining your goals. He or she may shed some light on what type of activity you need in order to reach a particular objective—especially if the person has some *experience* in achieving the results you're after.

For example, taking a shower and toweling off should not count as your daily exercise! Seriously, get some advice. The outside perspective can't hurt and will often help a great deal.

In the end, the bottom line to reaching your goals will be determined by your willingness to do the things you need to do, rather than those things you want to do. Take control of the baby steps to gain control of your future.

I can tell where you'll be
in five years
by watching you for 24 hours.

John C. Maxwell

Day 7

What are the Influences in Your Life?

I wrote much of this book at the libraries of three universities I attended. It caused me to reflect on 12 years of study. I never remember striving for excellence at any point in my college years, even though I considered additional schooling vital to my future. The conventional advice to "get an education and get a good job" still echoes in my head. To me, however, education meant a passing grade. That was all I wanted and that was all I received. Now I understand an "education" is much more.

Before extolling the virtues of an education, I would caution you, that the environment in which you receive the education, is probably more important. Your environment educates you 24 hours a day. You do not need to be enrolled in a course of study. Whether you are two or 82, your surroundings continually mold you.

So what type of environment do we place ourselves in? We have many to choose from, but often you will be encouraged to do what everyone else does. That's why I went to college. Everyone I knew was going. I got a job, because that's what everyone else did. I found myself doing what the masses of people were doing, and not really setting my own course. This can happen in a very slow and subtle way, to the point it isn't even noticeable.

So how does a person end up writing a book in the libraries of the universities he struggled in? Very simple, the environment changed. It wasn't that I put myself around literary giants, I just started listening to positive tapes, reading books and listening to possibility thinkers. Who would be more likely to tell you it's possible to play professional baseball; someone who never played professionally, or someone who had? The person who played professionally will *educate* you on the possibilities, because they know it's feasible. Chances are someone who has not played will inform you why you cannot.

I was around people who challenged me to generate positive energy in my life. The strange part was I didn't think I needed anything positive. I wasn't unhappy. In fact, I enjoyed my teaching career. When I started listening to positive tapes, and reading uplifting books, my view of the world changed. The world was the same, however, I began to change on the inside and look at things differently. I don't believe you have any concept of negative influences until you surround yourself with positive ones.

Negative Input

When was the last time you got up feeling inspired from watching television, or reading the newspaper? Networks battle for your time with different types of programming, much of it designed to persuade you into watching. The medical shows come up with the most amazing catastrophes ever experienced. The legal shows drum up scenarios in which people mistreat each other. Citizens are compensated to come go on air and share their dirty laundry in front of a live audience and millions of viewers. All this is dumped in your living room under the heading of "entertainment."

If you had been away from television for the past year, you would be startled at the programs you see today. A gradual numbing takes place as each program tries to top the one that came before it. Did you know a frog would remain in water and die, if the water is slowly brought to a boil? Yet, if you were to drop a frog in moderately hot water, the frog would leap out immediately. The same type of subtle warming is taking place on television. If you doubt this, put the television in the attic for a month. Everything will seem the same for the 30 days, until you watch it again. You will realize how much more productive you've been. I know this all sounds interesting (or for some of you annoying) to talk about, but the difference in your productivity and attitude will amaze you.

When you watch the news, read the newspaper, or get involved in break room gossip, does this help you? The theme always seems to be people's problems and what's wrong with the world. Why does this take priority over all the good things that are occurring? Quite simply, people don't want to hear about the good things. They would rather feel better by comparing their situation with someone else's problems, "Sure am glad I don't have their problems!"

The media and networks understand this. That's why they pipe in negative and tragedy, it makes people feel good by comparison. Moreover, in the long run, being more productive, financially, socially, spiritually etc., is what will make you feel good.

I know there are problems in the world, but how does soaking in them (real, or created for television) improve your future? Taking control of your environment will help you filter out the negative and create a consistent flow of positive energy into you day. Then, when your financial situation improves, you can help alleviate some of the problems other people are having.

You have a choice of what you watch and read. Therefore, you have a choice of the input you receive on a daily basis.

Positive Input

When you begin to identify some of the negative influences in your life, you can begin to eliminate, or at least neutralize their impact. As you can see in the following cartoon, the first block to fall is "positive input" which begins the chain reaction leading to "financial growth." Notice the size of each block grows-it needs the weight from the previous block, plus your effort, to knock it over. You cannot skip the process, walk to the last block, and knock it over; it's too big! Fighting this is a losing battle. I encourage you to embrace the process, and allow it to work in your life.

What goes in affects what comes out. You will be a product of your environment whether you like it or not. Take control of it, or it will continue to control you.

---

*The ancestor to every action
is a thought.*

Emerson

Day 8

Do You Belong in the Business World?

What do Phil Jackson, Scotty Bowman, Vince Lombardi, and Sparky Anderson all have in common? If you're not a sports fan, nothing! Stick with me anyway, as being a sports fan is not a pre-requisite to understanding my point.

Oddly enough, they all share two things. First, they are all considered the best, or one of the best, coaches of all time in their respective sports. Second, they were all average athletes. Of course, I use the word "average" in comparison to other professional athletes of their time. Let's analyze their careers.

The Player

❖ Phil Jackson (basketball)—Played 13 years, for the New York Knicks, 1969-1978, and the New Jersey Nets, 1978-1980; primarily as a reserve; 6.7 points and 4.3 rebounds per game. He played in 807 games.

❖ Scotty Bowman (hockey)—Played in the Quebec junior league (one step below the NHL in Canada) until a head injury ended his playing career in 1952 at the age of 18.

❖ Vince Lombardi (football)—Played guard for Fordham University, 1934-1936. Never played professionally as a player.

❖ Sparky Anderson (baseball)—Played second base in 1959 for the Philadelphia Phillies; career statistics: 152 games, .218 batting average, 0 home runs, 34 RBI (runs batted in).

All four of these men at one time played the sport that they eventually coached or managed in. As you can see the statistics are not overwhelming, but now let's contrast the numbers to their coaching records.

The Coach

❖ Phil Jackson—Coached Albany Patroons of the Continental Basketball Association, 1982-1987, record of 117-90 and won a league championship and coach of the year. Coached the Chicago Bulls, 1989-1998, and the Los Angeles Lakers 1999-2000; career record of 612-208, regular season, and 125-48, playoffs; *six NBA titles* with Chicago, and one thus far with the Lakers.

❖ Scotty Bowman—Career coaching record of 1144-538-295; 200 career playoff victories; *eight Stanley Cup Championships.* Coached for the St. Louis Blues, Montreal Canadiens, Pittsburgh Penguins, and Detroit Red Wings.

❖ Vince Lombardi—Green Bay Packers, 1959-1967; overall record was 141-39-4, for a winning percentage of .783. *Won five NFL championships*, including Super Bowl I and II. Voted into the Pro Football Hall of Fame in 1971.

❖ Sparky Anderson—Managed Cincinnati reds, 1970-1978, and Detroit Tigers, 1979-1995; career statistics: 2194-1834, regular season, won *four World Series titles* (three with Cincinnati and one with Detroit). Inducted into the Baseball Hall of Fame in 2000.

What jumps out in the comparisons? They did not have great careers or statistics as players, yet were able to coach a group of athletes to championship levels. It wasn't natural talent that made them great coaches, it was an ability to empower others. They generated a synergy in their players, which took them to the top of their respective sport as coaches. You may not consider yourself a "natural," but you can rise to great heights just as these four coaches did.

I bring this to your attention because too many people write themselves off, as if success were something only another person could attain. The fact that these four became great coaches was no fluke. I am sure they worked very hard. The path they took is also available to you.

Extraordinary people can be "ordinary" people who do something "extra."

I hope, as you look at the contrast from player to coach of these four men, it will allow you to at least think of the possibility of doing something extraordinary with your life as well. You may already have accomplished that level as a friend, parent, or spouse. Why not in the business world? There's no limit to what one inspired person can accomplish.

Day 9

Separate Your Meetings

Can the way we view a meeting determine the outcome? In my humble opinion, I would say there's little doubt it can.

Suppose you're making three sales calls on the same day. You walk in for your first appointment with a big smile on your face. The problem is, however, the person who sounded so excited about meeting with you has reconsidered. It had nothing to do with you, but for some reason your prospect has gone belly up! The meeting was cancelled without notification or explanation.

The next appointment at least showed up, but based on the result, perhaps it would have been better if they hadn't. Appointment number three is at the end of the day, so you wallowed in the two failures for three hours. When you started the third meeting, you noticed the enthusiasm had left your voice. You're certain the prospect picked up on it, which caused you to start pressing. You felt like a mechanical robot pelting out facts and figures until you weren't even sure what you were talking about! Sure enough, no "sale."

You became discouraged and analyzed every move of the day, "would've" "could've," and "should've" were playing a chorus in your mind.

If you're in a business that deals with people, you have most likely had days like this. The key element of the day is not what went wrong with the meetings; it's how you handled what went wrong.

What if your first meeting (with a company or prospect) had an unexpected financial problem. If that were the case, that is totally out of your control. Yes, it affected your appointment, but there's nothing you could've done about it.

Is it possible your disappointment from the first meeting affected the way you viewed the next two? I can tell you this has happened to me more than once. When the edge comes off just a little, people will notice. Even more important, you notice!

This is tough medicine, but when you allow factors out of your control to dampen your enthusiasm, you are not in charge. Bad meetings and cancellations only affect your attitude if you allow them to. This is much easier to write about than it is to live, but it is the truth. People and companies have bad days, and they will disappoint you now and then. You need to remain focused on what you can control. People should get your best, regardless of whether your previous meeting went well or not. Sometimes you are on the brink of success and don't even know it. On the following page, one more dig—in the cartoon—and he'll hit pay dirt!

What We Can Control

There are three components to a successful meeting. First, you need to find the right person for your product or service. They need to be looking for whatever it is you're offering (you would not sell ice to an Eskimo!). Second, you need to find that person at the right time in their life. The individual or company may be looking for what you have, but not be in a position to utilize or purchase it right now. The third part of the equation would be sharing what you have with the right attitude. Of the three, there is only one you control—your attitude.

Therefore, it's the one we need to work on and keep positive at all times. Another benefit to having a positive attitude is the possibility of referrals. Even if your prospect is not interested, they can always connect you with someone they know, who might be. In fact, since they probably have a better idea of your product or service after meeting with you, they may refer a "tailor made" prospect. The impression you make in your meeting will often determine whether you are referred to someone with a stamp of approval.

Each person you meet with can either be a source of business or a source of prospects. Therefore, even when people are not ready or interested in what you're selling, they can be a reservoir of potential contacts. Giving a positive and professional presentation will improve the likelihood of a steady flow of referrals. The more referrals you obtain, the more meetings you'll have. This will lead to more business.

I refer to this as "flipping stones." Eventually you'll find something underneath one. Rather than looking under one, wishing there were something beneath it, why not flip another one until you find someone to work with?

If you've never asked for a referral before, you'll be shocked when the question comes out of your mouth the first time. You'll be thinking, "Where did those words come from?" It is so simple, yet so difficult to do the first time. After a few attempts, however, it'll be a natural part of your meetings. When the world of referrals opens up, you will not need any one person, as your list of names becomes bottomless! When your prospect senses he's not the only person on the planet to whom you're talking, he looks at your presentation for his benefit, not yours.

Instead of selling, you will be sorting! There's an endless supply of people out there, the more people you go through with a positive upbeat attitude, the more success you'll see. Other than making the appointment, you control only the italicized in the following chart.

Equation	Result
Right person + wrong time + *wrong attitude* =	"No"
Wrong person + right time + *wrong attitude* =	"No"
Right person + right time + *wrong attitude* =	"No"
Right person + wrong time + *right attitude* =	"Maybe later"/referral
Wrong person + right time + *right attitude* =	Referral
Wrong person + wrong time + *right attitude* =	Referral
Right person + right time + *right attitude* =	*Bingo*!

Many potential business partners and sales are left on the table, because people are afraid to ask the "closing" question. For instance, if you wanted to get someone interested in a business opportunity, you could explain all the benefits of the business with incredible enthusiasm. However, if you never ask them to get involved, they may never make a decision. Even if they're interested, sometimes you have to help people make decisions by simply asking a question, such as, *"Let's work on this together, I think we could make a lot of money together!"* Or, *"Lets write up this policy for you, it's obvious we can save you some money while increasing your benefits."*

Each of these statements describes the benefits, while asking a question that requires a "yes" or "no" answer. If you never ask, you may never know!

Our doubts are traitors,
and make us lose the good
we oft might win,
by fearing to attempt.

William Shakespeare

Day 10

Your Guardian Angel

There's a wonderful story from many years ago about a mule and a caravan. An entire town was moving from their home, looking for greener pastures and a fresh start. One of the challenges they encountered was the road out of town. It was very narrow. This did not deter the group however, as they would find a better life waiting for them in the new city. So a little inconvenience on the trip was not of big concern, they would just travel slowly.

All packed up, they began the 200-mile trip to their new home. There were hundreds of people, so the journey would not be an easy one. About 100 miles into their journey, they came across a large mule in the middle of the road blocking their way. They did everything in their power to move this mule, as there was no way of traveling around it. For hours the leaders of this caravan attempted to get the mule out of the road. All attempts of force failed.

They had never encountered such a stubborn animal anywhere, and frustration began to take over. The weather turned bad, as pouring rain and wind started making matters worse. They were at their wits end as the mule refused to move. Everyone was angry and nobody could understand. Certainly they knew mules were stubborn, but this one was acting as if it meant to block their way. Not one person could find a good thing to say. Half a day was wasted sitting in the rain, while everyone discussed their misfortune, wondering why this was happening to them.

Finally, the mule decided he had been there long enough and went on his way, much to the delight of the caravan. The weather had improved, although the road had turned muddy and the trip would take longer than anticipated. They had not figured on such a delay, and provisions for the trip would be a bit short. Nothing to be overly concerned with, but when you consider the weather, and everyone's bad attitude about the delay, this was an added frustration the group didn't need.

A day later, the caravan finally could see their destination ahead. Tired and hungry, the journey was finally over. As they approached the town, however, something was terribly wrong with the city they had heard so much about. It was in ruins. A storm had whipped through the town and destroyed almost everything standing.

If not for the mule in the road, the caravan would have arrived at precisely the same time as the storm. What appeared to be an untimely delay and inconvenience may have saved their lives. Who knows what might have happened if they'd arrived earlier. Could it be there was a guardian angel looking out for these travelers, who placed the mule in the road to spare them from the disastrous storm?

You, too, may have a guardian angel looking out for you, because you have made it through your life this far! All the untimely interruptions to your day—airport delays, road construction, long checkout lines at the grocery store, traffic jams—may have, in effect, kept you out of harm's way. Do you look at obstacles in your life this way? Most people don't. They often let their frustration get the best of them.

Next time something has the appearance of going against you, perhaps you should give some thought to that guardian angel looking out for you. It may allow you to relax a little, and make the best of a troublesome circumstance. Sometimes a situation is only there to prevent another one that could be even more damaging to you. Perhaps it's there to make you take notice of something in your life that needs attending. The expression "everything happens for a reason" can be comforting if you allow it to be.

Maybe it's a bit of a stretch to ask you to be thankful for that "cancelled" sign at the airport terminal, or that traffic jam on the way to work. However, before you let it agitate you too much, consider that it may be keeping you out of harms way, or keeping you in a place where something wonderful is about to happen.

When one door of happiness closes,
another opens, but often we look so long
at the closed door that we do not see
the one that has been opened for us.

Helen Keller

Look the Part

Your appearance speaks before you say a word. It is the first line of communication, and creates the first impression people have of you. This is a double edge sword; it can cut for, or against you. If you went to an accountant for the first time and they were wearing nothing but jeans and a t-shirt, would you make a judgment about them? Before you knew anything about their ability or background, wouldn't you question it? Not that you plan to, as in "I wonder how they'll be dressed?" Yet, what they wear affects you instantly.

If you've ever gone to a job interview, didn't you double check your appearance? Every time you meet a new person, you're interviewing. It may not be fair, but it happens, so you should use it to your advantage.

Dress will also represent you to yourself. If you want to feel sharp, you need to look sharp. If you want to feel like an executive or salesperson, you need to look like one. Looking important helps you think important. If you are starting out in the business world for the first time, or a veteran for that matter, find someone you respect and ask for some help (yes, there's that mentor thing again!). Ask if they have any suggestions about improving your dress.

One business consultant I spoke with made this suggestion to me, "Pay twice as much and buy half as many." Quality will go a lot farther than quantity. There is nothing wrong with wearing the same clothes frequently, provided you are meeting with different prospects each time. Quality clothing will take the pounding of constant use. Eventually, you'll have the money to sink into clothes. If you need to cut corners, do so on the quantity.

Be wary of getting initial advice at a clothing store. Remember, most salespeople work on commission and would like to sell you all kinds of clothes. Have a good idea of what you're looking for before going to a retailer. This way you can get the retailer's guidance, by placing it within an educated parameter that you set.

A successful message, one of conviction and belief, comes through your eyes. If someone is too busy noticing your dress, they never catch that message. You may not like it, you may not agree with it, but dress is vital to communicating effectively.

I am not an expert on business dress, but I understand the value of consulting with one. There are different styles of dress based on climate and time of year. Make it a priority to get some industry-specific counsel on appropriate dress for your industry.

Make sure you look your best. Dress right. You can't afford not to!

Straighten Up

I hope that you have an area that you can refer to as an office. Even if you don't, by all means clean up the area where you conduct your business. You do not want crumpled-up papers, old business cards, plates with sandwich crumbs, cans and bottles, receipts, or thousands of pieces of paper with notes scribbled on them (of course that's not my office!), surrounding you as you attempt to conduct business—especially when you are making phone calls.

There was a time when I found things in my office by section and layer number! (You know, "did I put that number in this pile, or the one on the floor?") When I finally organized everything, it amazed me how much better I felt in my office.

A crisp and clean environment is important if you're attempting to communicate enthusiastically with another person. Placing a few plaques on the wall with success principle would help as well. Another good idea might be to surround yourself with some of the dreams and goals you have for you and your family. Get some vacation pictures out, or maybe a couple posters of your dream car. It will not take much time to clean and/or decorate your office space, but it will help you focus.

If you are questioning the importance of office cleanliness, take an hour to clean up. If you don't notice the difference, just throw everything right back where it was!

Long before I am near enough to talk to you on the street, in a meeting or at a party, you announce your sex, age, and class to me through what you are wearing and very possibly give me important information (or misinformation) as to your occupation, origin, personality, opinions, tastes, and current mood. By the time we meet and converse, we have already spoken to each other in an older and more universal voice.

**Allison Lurie,
author of *The Language of Clothes***

Day 12

Understanding Others

A key element in communicating effectively is taking the time to grasp the perspective of the other person. Before you can guide or influence someone, it helps to know where they're coming from. There's always another perspective, even if you fail to recognize it. Taking the time to listen can set the stage for a productive two-way conversation.

Picture two blindfolded people touching and describing an elephant (as I jump right into a bizarre example!). One person may be touching the tusk, "smooth and slick." The other individual may be touching the side, "rough and flat." They are both touching and describing the same animal, but each has a different perspective—and neither one is wrong. Do you see where confrontation could occur without further information? Here would be a good place for saying something like, "I feel a smooth, slick surface, what do you feel?" The other person would counter, "I feel something rough and flat, I wonder why that is?"

Eventually through a series of questions and feedback, each would discover they are just touching a different part of the animal. They could discover this by talking; opening their eyes would not be necessary. It's difficult to be aware of all the potential differences you may have with other people. If you listen, however, and make an effort to understand, you may find yourself communicating and learning at the same time—a powerful combination! When someone else is talking, are you listening, or waiting for them to finish so you can speak?

Communication begins with an awareness that another perspective exists. That other perspective can only become apparent if you allow the other person to share it. The cliché, "There are two sides to every story," will serve you well if you allow it to.

Consider two automobiles approaching an intersection at the same time. The light is red for one car, and green for the other. If the vehicle having the right of way proceeds without paying attention the other vehicle, you may have an accident. If the driver coming the other way does not notice their red light, you may collide. Never assume that because you think you're right everyone else will see it that way. In driving through an intersection, you should always take into account another driver's perspective to avoid collisions. As we can see below, the fact he was right means little when on his way to the hospital.

Realize you won't agree with another person's perspective all the time; you should hold strong to your beliefs. However, don't assume everyone views things in the same way. You can avoid "accidents" communicating with people, especially for the first time, by being observant (look both ways!), and alert to different points of view.

While on the subject of driving, remember a red light *never* stopped an automobile—always look both ways!

People Don't Care How Much You Know Until They Know How Much You Care

A successful businessman (we'll call him Jim) shared a story with me that taught him this lesson early in his career. Jim had a breakfast meeting with a local business owner to share a marketing business. If you were to stack all the trends in business into one pile, Jim had everything on his side; like a bazooka shooting a mosquito!

Jim unloaded all his information on his prospect for about a half hour. After which the prospect asked him a few simple questions, "Do you know what I do for a living?" and "Do you know how many kids I have?" Jim did not know the answers, or understand the nature of the questions. That is, until the prospect pointed out he had no interest getting in business with someone who did not take an interest in him personally.

Jim told me what a humbling experience that was for him and also how fortunate he was to have this prospect be honest with him. He learned a valuable lesson that day, one we can all learn from. Take the time to listen and ask questions. Find out about people and their views on subjects before pouring all your knowledge out. I once heard it put quite simply, "Seek first to understand and then be understood."

The Dead Air Test

A good way to analyze your listening skills might be to notice moments in your conversations where nobody is talking. If you are the first one to talk all the time, you perhaps need work on your listening skills. Realize you learn very little when you're talking, but a whole lot when you are listening. Ask questions, and listen to the answers. This will put you on solid ground in a conversation, and allow you to have more influence when you do give information or opinions. People love it when they are allowed to share their beliefs to a captive audience.

If you feel you are struggling to listen, it may have something to do with your confidence. Often times, when we pile on information to prove a point, we're not so sure about ourselves. Do you ever feel like you said something that did not register with the person you're talking to? I know I have. Then I say the same thing in a different way, trying to prove a point I already stated. That's when I get that "I'm piling on too much information" feeling that comes from talking too much. Lack of confidence can be in the idea you're proposing, or in yourself. The good news is, you can fix that!

You will notice, the more confidence you have, the more listening you do. The more listening you do, the more influential you are with people. Therefore, before you get caught up in a "new" listening technique, don't forget it all begins with you and your confidence.

---

*It's surprising
how many persons
go through life
without ever recognizing that
their feelings toward other people
are largely determined
by their feelings toward themselves,
and if you're not
comfortable within yourself,
you can't be
comfortable with others.*

Sidney Harris

Day 13

Alex

Alex, another student with whom I worked, was non-verbal, so understanding him was difficult at times, but he always got his point across. He was mild mannered and in good spirits nearly all the time. Then his demeanor changed. Alex stopped eating many of his favorite foods. He was having mood swings at lunch on a regular basis. He always enjoyed ice cream, but now wouldn't touch it. A once healthy appetite was reduced to nibbling.

Then the problems spilled into other areas of his life. Gym and art class became challenging. Everything was suddenly a struggle in his life. He began to exhibit behavior we had never seen before.

We attempted to put Alex on some behavioral modification programs. These were designed to create "acceptable" behavior, since his actions were outside the parameters of what we defined as satisfactory. Notice the phrase "we defined." Our behavior programs (an attempt to communicate to Alex what we wanted) made things worse. The harder we tried to get Alex to behave the way we wanted him to, the worse things got.

As it turns out, during a routine visit, the dentist found a tooth that had to be extracted. There were signs Alex had a dental problem, as everything started when he was eating food. Unfortunately, we focused on getting him to behave a certain way, which only made things worse.

The communication (bad behavior) from Alex was there. We just didn't recognize it. We were hacking at the leaves and the problem was in the roots. As a side note, recall I mentioned there were problems in gym class? He was responding to us in a negative manner all day, not just when eating. Alex became confrontational because we were trying to mold his behavior, rather than understand it. In essence, we built a wall between us in all his classes, which had nothing to do with the original situation (problems at lunch).

Think of the troubles you have had with people. Often you can trace them back to one miscommunication, which established a permanent wall in all your dealings with one another. Perhaps it is time to start understanding the origin of the wall, instead of banging your head into it.

Beware the Minefields

I recall sitting around a table with a group of people when the word "retarded" popped up to describe someone's actions. The word was said in jest, but it created quite a bit of tension. Not because of the teasing nature of the comment, but because the word was used in a mocking tone.

When you use a word such as this in a mocking manner with anyone in the field of education, or who has a friend or family member with special needs, you will invariably offend them. This of course is not your intention. Describing someone as "retarded" is no different than describing someone as having blue eyes or learning disabilities. Retardation is a characteristic someone is born with completely out of his or her control. However, a demeaning context, or mocking tone changes the impact of the term completely.

I bring this up not to scold people who have used this word (although I would hope those who do would now think twice), but to shed light on the potential pitfalls, which can occur when communicating with others.

Three people were offended by the use of the word that day, despite knowing it was not said to offend anyone. Rather than getting upset, an explanation as to why the particular use of such a label was inappropriate would have done the trick.

The lack of communication went both ways really, as everyone could have learned a little bit more about understanding other people's perspectives. Remember there is a difference between stupidity and ignorance. Information will cure ignorance and it can be given in a peaceful manner.

---

*By union the
smallest states thrive.
By discord the
greatest are
destroyed.*

Sallust

Day 14

Take Responsibility

Taking responsibility, now there's a tough one. The difficulty in taking responsibility is that you first must recognize your part. I was frequently frustrated as an employee when I was teaching. I always thought I was underpaid for the work and time I put in. Do you ever feel that way? Well, let's look at it through the eyes of responsibility.

The possibility exists, if you do not face and overcome your fears (like the telephone), that someone who has overcome their fears will control your finances and to a certain extent, your life. Now, before that statement offends you, think about it for a moment.

It takes courage to go out and start your own company. If you are receiving a paycheck with someone else's signature on it, that person took all the risk. If you lose a job, you go get another one. If someone loses a business, they often loose everything they own! My point is not to condemn hard working people with jobs, only to point out the inherent dangers of relying on a paycheck for your sole source of income.

For years, I put the finances of my life in someone else's hands. It was easy to pass on that responsibility because for the most part a pay scale is pre-determined. My paycheck was based on showing up for work, more than it was on performance. Then I realized, without the ability to control my income through performance, I was giving the responsibility to someone else. You can scream foul, blame the "system" all you want, but every time you point a finger, there's three coming back at you.

That realization was like eating spinach (which I hate by the way!), but it wasn't until I faced it that my financial situation changed. You have all the opportunity in the world to become self-employed and run your own business. Yet, most people work for someone else. Did you know you are four times more likely to become a millionaire if you were born outside the borders of North

America? That is one scary statistic! It tells me the land of opportunity is here right in front of our faces. Yet how many of us take advantage of what we have.

Nobody is suggesting you shouldn't get frustrated about what you're paid, or asked to do, at work. Only that you channel that frustration to the ultimately responsible party—you!

Temper

You can tell the size of the person, by the size of that which makes them upset. That just about says it all!

People are always blaming
their circumstances
for what they are.
I don't believe in circumstances.
The people who get on
in this world are the people
who get up and look for
the circumstances they want,
and, if they can't find them,
make them.

George Bernard Shaw

Day 15

Be Excited about What You Do

What happens when you put a "zero" in the sales column of a company's financial statement? No other columns have any real meaning with a zero for sales. Do you see a need for managers? Factory workers? Maintenance people? Secretaries? Vice presidents? Most people you know, currently working for or running a company, owe their income to sales.

Appreciate the important role sales play in generating revenue for a company. I would hope you feel enthusiastic about going out there setting up sales, or developing business partners. The bottom line—*sales* make the business world go!

Your attitude about your product or service is one thing, but just as important is the way you see your industry. In many cases, we let other people determine our perspective on what we do for a living. The moment a negative comment is directed at you, it registers inside. Regardless of how "tough" you are. You can't change everyone who thinks differently than you, so don't allow their opinion to control your reality. Usually ignorance keeps people from understanding what you're trying to accomplish. Consider them misinformed and continue pursuing your vision. In the end, if you allow someone else's attitude to slow you down—then their opinion counts more than yours!

Enthusiasm and the Computer

There are quite a few people looking to create wealth sitting behind a computer. This may happen, but for the average person starting a new company or product line, this thinking may be a mistake.

Ask someone who has succeeded at any venture how important enthusiasm is. You will find most rank it at, or near, the top. Even the quietest person can emanate enthusiasm through their personality. When someone is excited, it jumps out through their body language, voice, and eyes. Technology will support, but not replace, your enthusiasm.

Where does the enthusiasm come from on the computer? Very simple, the exclamation point (!) at the end of a sentence. I would put my money on you and your excitement, before that little symbol on the keyboard.

Concerns for man and his fate
must always form
the chief interest
of all technical endeavors.
Never forget this in the midst
of your diagrams
and equations.

Albert Einstein

Day 16

Stan

Have you ever wondered what it takes to get someone to a new level of performance?

Each of us has people in our lives we influence. In fact, you probably influence people several times a day without even knowing it. The manner in which you handle yourself, the words you use, even the jokes you tell, all speak very loudly. Actually, you are a walking talking advertisement of who you are on a daily basis. Moreover, who you are, determines the type of influence, positive or negative, that you have on other people. The environment you create for others, therefore, can literally change their lives.

To give you a good example of this principle, I'd like to share a situation we encountered with a student named Stan. He had special needs, just as we all do (do you do your own taxes, fly your own airplane, do your own physical?). In particular, Stan had a need for a fresh start. He had a few bad work experiences that really had him down. Stan's self esteem was really in need of a boost.

The previous work experiences were so negative in fact; someone (a job coach) had to go with Stan to any work setting. There were plenty of stories about his challenges from other schools he had worked with. The stories were tough to avoid, as they were documented and deemed "necessary" information when preparing his new work setting. The reports were designed to inform us of his history, so we knew what to expect.

When Stan started a new job (at a local university), we never read the reports. To get Stan to a higher level of confidence and independence, we decided to start with a clean slate. There was no need for pre-conceived expectations about potential problems.

Stan became comfortable with our agency and got to know everyone over time. He soon became known as "smiling Stan." The first few days of work are always a bit nerve racking, for both the job coach and student. Heaping *praise* on Stan was the first order of business—not finding fault with his shortcomings. We wanted Stan to feel encouraged and comfortable, not scrutinized. Empowering him to perform to the best of his ability was our focus. Stan wanted his independence right away, but the state required someone from the agency to stay close by for the first few weeks. This allowed us to gain some insight into his behavior in the new work environment.

One day, on the way to work, Stan heard these magical words, "We believe in you." We told him it was time for him to work on his own—and that the agency supervision would be in an adjacent room, rather than over his shoulder. The smile was so big you could have driven a truck through it! We told Stan we believed he was capable of working on his own and that everyone had confidence in him. Based on this confidence, he earned his independence. Eventually, Stan worked his shift entirely by himself—and even took the bus on his own. The confidence we placed in Stan started a momentum in his life that we could not explain.

He far exceeded any level of independence from earlier work settings. His behavior at work was excellent and he became a very popular worker at the school. He was a beaming, independent member of the work force. The previous experiences did not have to determine Stan's future results. Stan had corrected his shortcomings, because he was encouraged and allowed to do so.

This theory may help, should you aspire to a position of leadership. Setting expectations based on past performance may hinder your ability to enhance an individual's future.

We all learned a valuable lesson from working with Stan; praising progress will do more for someone than correcting their past. Therein lies a secret to empowering others, build the person, and the person will build their future.

Never punish a learner.

Ken Blanchard

Day 17

Take Care of Yourself

Chances are, you already know what you need to do, or what you need to cut out to improve your health. Interestingly enough, many people have no idea how much better they would feel with just moderate attention to diet and exercise. Sure, we all think it would be nice to be in better physical shape, but do we really know what it would be like?

When you get tired during the day, do you brush it off as working too hard? Do you blame lethargy on getting old? If so, you are relegating yourself to "victim" status. Obviously, you can't change the fact you're getting older, but it makes a good excuse for being too tired. When you're too tired to exercise, you eliminate one of the best ways to get your energy back—exercise! Couple a little exercise with some better eating habits, and you'll be on your way.

I am not going to suggest you eat like a rabbit and exercise like you're training for the Olympics, but a few subtle habits incorporated into your life can have a huge impact on your strength and stamina.

A question people find themselves asking is, "Should I go on a diet and exercise program, or not?" Actually, if you have to go on a "program," that's the biggest part of the problem. Ideally, establishing positive routines that become part of your life will enable you to stay in good health, and be happy about it! Any change you make, like a little exercise first thing in the morning, will seem like a program for awhile, but the goal is to make it part of your normal routine, just like brushing your teeth!

The first place to start is with a professional such as a nutritionist, fitness trainer, or physician. They can give you the professional counsel you need to set a course of action that best fits your needs. However, ultimately it's up to you to make the necessary changes.

A reason to make positive changes in your habits is a great place to begin. For example, people often want to know *how* to stop smoking. There are so many methods it would be difficult to list them all. The simple way to quit smoking is to stop putting the cigarette in your mouth! That is truly the way to stop smoking, is it not? Until you have a reason *why* you should stop, knowing how may not help.

I am not picking on smokers, only using it as an example. First, attempt to figure out *why* you want to change, before getting all caught up in "how to." When your reason is strong enough, just about any method will work. The "how vs. why" theme is at work in your health, as well as your business life.

Hopefully you won't wait until a professional gives you a directive which contains the words "or else." Be proactive, and start making some changes to put you on track to a healthier lifestyle.

If all you did was exercise 15 minutes a day, and moderate the foods you eat too much of, your energy level will grow and in time you will look and feel much better. At some point, standing in a line at lunch and simply barking out "Number 5 and hold the pickles" gets old. When you start to realize the benefits of small changes, perhaps you will make bigger ones.

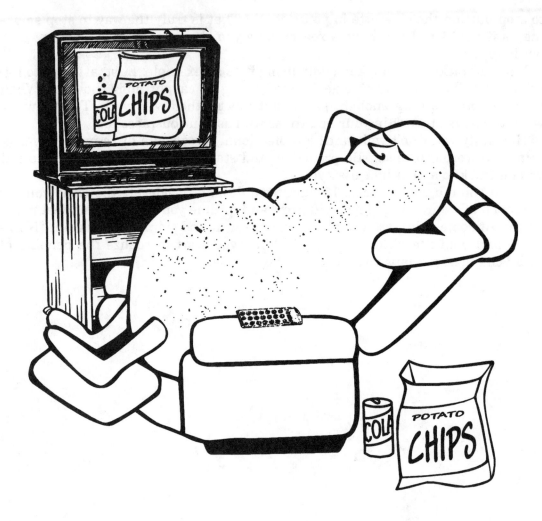

Day 18

Be Aware of the Emotional Rollercoaster

There's an important period of time for someone when they add something new to their life or schedule. It may vary, but usually people are very fragile in the first 30 days. They have just injected another item into what is probably a busy schedule, and this can create a brittle attitude.

For example, suppose I show a business opportunity to Bill. After about 30 minutes of discussion, he seems to grasp the concept. We talk about the benefits of the business model, but somehow Bill seems more interested in the mechanics (as most people are in the beginning). We part company, and Bill is excited about everything. Of course, I am excited because Bill is saying all the right things, which leads me to believe I have been very convincing.

Often times, however, Bill will begin discussing with someone else what he has just seen. This is where the danger begins. Bill walked away with your logic fully ingrained in his head, but there's a good chance the first thing to hit him afterwards is an emotional punch. In other words, someone challenged Bill on what he believed to be true. What happens when Bill gets such an opinion from someone he respects? He may start to doubt his judgment, or worse yet, wonder if I gave him the straight scoop. Questions about time, money, and legitimacy may begin twirling through his mind. Those are all legitimate concerns to Bill, or anyone for that matter.

That is why I encourage you to spend some time with every potential customer or client on *why* they should use your product or service. We are creatures of emotion, not logic. There's several scenarios people could face: Their best friend or family may not buy into the idea, or vision they have for it. Someone they talk to could provide misinformation, which they trust, because the individual giving that advice may have good intentions, even if they are wrong.

When this happens, people will often come back and simply have an excuse to not pursue any further dealings with you. It has been my experience the excuse is buried in emotion, not fact. Once hit with a little doubt, rationalizations get involved such as lack of time or money. Either way, you are stuck with a person whose tail is between his or her legs.

If all we do is ride the emotions of a positive meeting, a crash could be just around the corner. I am not suggesting we dampen someone's enthusiasm. Nevertheless, you can at least prepare him or her for the possibility before it occurs. I share from my experience, a few examples of what they can expect before we talk again. Therefore, when and if something occurs, I will actually gain credibility in their eyes. Rather than an excuse, I will usually get a "How did you know that?" Preparing people for potential ups and downs is not dampening enthusiasm; it's just common sense. Be the seat belt for people who are about to go on an emotional roller coaster.

Attempt to handle objections before they come up whenever possible. It's a matter of helping people find solutions to challenges, rather than giving in to them.

The things which hurt,
instruct.

Benjamin Franklin

Day 19

Brett

In my early days as a teacher, I had the good fortune of working with an experienced and knowledgeable supervisor named Dennis. He was not a "by the book" type of person, as the book was never present when dealing with one of his students. Dennis had some schooling, but it was his insight into human behavior that was so powerful. He looked at each individual and situation as unique. Yet, he understood some fundamental values that applied to everybody. In his view, the most important of these was the need to be self-determining. I mention Dennis to let you know his influence was responsible for the way I looked at this next situation.

Brett was a very quiet young man, but often would act up a bit when things were not going the way he wanted. We were on a field trip one afternoon, eating in a crowded restaurant, when Brett suddenly decided to drop to the floor. He was a big kid, so when he decided to do something like this, it was difficult to prevent. I was not in the restaurant at the time, but entered about five minutes later. Numerous attempts had been made to get Brett off the floor. He was very content down there, and the harder people tried to get him up, the more he resisted. When I reached him, instead of asking him to get up off the floor, I asked him how he was doing and patted him on the shoulder. After about a minute, I leaned over and whispered in his ear, "When you're ready to get up Brett, you can." About five seconds later he got up and went back to his table.

All Brett wanted was recognition that he had some control over what happened in his life. Whispering it in his ear kept the statement very private, so Brett could let it be known it was his decision to go back to his seat. All the convincing in the world, or promises of what he could have, meant nothing. When he was given control, he decided it was time to get up. The control was his all the time, and when others attempted to take it, the situation did not improve.

I had seen Dennis do this with several students in previous years, so Brett getting off the floor was not that miraculous to me. The most telling part of the story is that many present did not believe it. With all the data and programming available for behavior problems in our students, how could it all boil down to something so basic?

Fortunately, that's a question for someone else, I only know that it does. I do my best to take that teaching and insight with me wherever I go. It applies to Brett. Does it apply to the people you deal with everyday?

For example, it could be as simple as asking a question instead of making a demand. Suppose you want your child to clean their room. You could say, "Are you cleaning your room now, or before lunch?" The fact that the room is to be cleaned is understood, but the control of the situation belongs to your child. They have a choice and some control.

If they do not follow through before lunch, which sounds better, "Clean your room!" or "You told me you would clean your room?" The worst-case scenario would be, should you need to be more forceful, make them follow through on something they said, rather than something you told them to do.

I know there are moments when your kids need to be told what to do, but the point remains, give some control and people will respond.

Take Time for Yourself and Family

When you break down the word recreation, you can see the phrase "re-create." How many people have you seen out on the golf course, act like they just lost their life savings when they miss a putt, or drive the golf ball into the water? That person is not re-creating, they are raising their blood pressure.

The idea is to relax, unwind, and give yourself a break from the daily grind. The tension can catch up to you emotionally if you're not careful.

A recreational activity could be having a cup of coffee with your spouse, watching a movie, reading a book, going for a walk; actually, it could be anything that gives your mind and body a break. If you don't think you need something like that in your life, perhaps you should seek a second opinion? Ask someone who will give you an honest answer and you may be surprised at what you hear. The individual who doesn't think they need time to relax is often the one who needs it the most.

Before you sense I am getting carried away with the idea of recreation every-day, I don't think missing a staff meeting because you were playing horseshoes is a good idea! Your commitments will probably vary on a daily basis, but try incorporating something daily, that allows you to step back and relax. For example, I go to the gym several times a week. I certainly get my exercise, but I do not enjoy going. Therefore, I do not consider a trip to the gym as recreation. The way you feel about an activity will determine how relaxing it is.

I don't mean to pick on all the golfers out there, but if you can go golfing without wrapping a club around a tree, great! Oddly enough, I was golfing not too long ago and saw a gentleman hit his tee shot into a pond. The recreation for me came when he threw his club in moments later!

Many of you reading this book have visions of "permanent" recreation when your income grows. Recreation can help you get there quicker, by increasing your effectiveness.

It can energize and refresh your attitude. You will be more equipped to deal with your day, when you have given your mind and body some time to relax. So kick back and have some fun once in awhile, it will pay off in your finances and your long-term health.

Day
21

Faith

Is there a topic that evokes more emotion in people than faith? I do not feel the necessity to get into the specifics of my own faith, but I did want to include the subject. One of the most powerful statements I ever heard was by a man named John Crowe who said, "Success is not for people of a particular faith, it's for people of good faith."

So much of what we do and hear today has to be "politically correct." What do politics have to do with it? My faith did not develop when I was younger, because like a typical kid, I avoided all the things my parents made me do. As I got older, I started to ask questions. Perhaps that's all I can encourage you to do.

Too often people wait for something dramatic to occur before they start asking questions. I think you'll find a strong faith can energize every facet of your life. I hope you have, or are willing to go in search of, that "good faith" and nourish it.

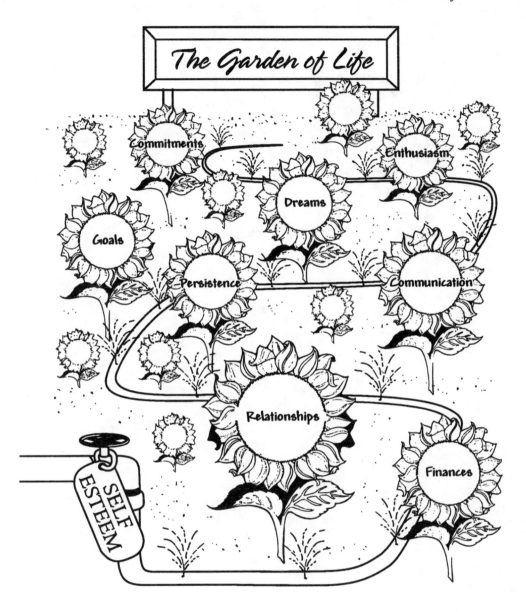

The Garden of Life

Personal Checklist

Ability to set up appointments on by phone? ____

1. Poor
2. Fair
3. Good
4. Excellent

Ability to set goals? ____

1. Poor
2. Fair
3. Good
4. Excellent

Ability to reach goals? ____

1. Poor
2. Fair
3. Good
4. Excellent

Attitude about my future financial situation? ____

1. Poor
2. Fair
3. Good
4. Excellent

My leisure time? ____

1. Do not enjoy it
2. It's okay
3. Very relaxing

Contacting on the phone? ____

1. Scares me to death
2. Will not touch it
3. Bothers me, but I use it anyway
4. Doesn't bother me at all

I read positive books ____

1. Never
2. Seldom
3. Sometimes
4. Always

I listen to positive tapes ____

1. Never
2. Seldom
3. Sometimes
4. Always

I have a "spring" in my step at work? ____

1. Never
2. Seldom
3. Sometimes
4. Always

Teamwork is important? ____

1. Never
2. Seldom
3. Sometimes
4. Always

Counsel from others is important? ____

1. No
2. Sometimes
3. Yes

The phone is a cashbox for my future? ____

1. No
2. Yes

Total score part I _____
Total score part II _____

The increase in your score may not represent financial growth just yet. However, it represents something much more important—personal growth. The money and lifestyle you create will be a by-product of your personal development. Keep working on yourself and good things are just around the corner. Congratulations on the completion of your *Check Mark Program*!

Conclusion

I hope that you are reading this having successfully completed the 21-day program. It is also my hope you have learned a few things about yourself and the potential that lies within you.

There is no substitute for the self-confidence personal performance develops. It is difficult to explain, but if you have just finished the 21 days of this program, you know exactly what I'm referring to. It's easy to begin, but the true test is in finishing. The confidence you have will spill into everything you do, and the people around you will sense it. You'll feel less dependent on getting the good "breaks," because deep down, you know you can make your own.

Couple that confidence with a true desire to enhance and serve other people and there's nothing you can't accomplish. Zig Ziglar says, "Help enough other people get what they want, and you'll get what you want." That perspective is important, as you want to channel your newfound belief in the right direction.

I have enjoyed sharing some thoughts and perspectives with you, and wish you nothing but the best in your future.

Recommended Reading

The Magic Of Thinking Big, David J. Schwartz
How To Win Friends And Influence People, Dale Carnegie
Skill With People, Les Giblin
The 7 Habits of Highly Effective People, Steven R. Covey
The Choice, Og Mandino
The Greatest Miracle In The World, Og Mandino
Born To Win, Lewis Timberlake
You And Your Network, Fred Smith
Think And Grow Rich, Napoleon Hill
Wake Up Calls, Eric Allenbaugh
The 21 Irrefutable Laws Of Leadership, John C. Maxwell
The Winner Within, Pat Riley
Rich Dad, Poor Dad, Robert T. Kiyosaki
Seeds Of Greatness, Dennis Waitley

Recommended Tapes

Listed by speaker name only-each has several cassette tapes available

Zig Ziglar
Dale Carnegie (Carnegie & Associates)
Dennis Waitley
John C. Maxwell
Les Brown
Brian Tracey
Steven Covey
Suze Orman
Rick Pitino
Norman Vincent Peale
Rita Davenport
Robert T. Kiyosaki